Fingernails Across the Chalkboard

Fingernails Across the Chalkboard

Poetry and Prose on HIV/AIDS from the Black Diaspora

Edited by
Randall Horton
M. L. Hunter
Becky Thompson

With a Foreword by Haki R. Madhubuti

Third World Press
Chicago, IL

Third World Press
Publishers since 1967
Chicago

First Edition
Printed in the United States of America

12 11 10 09 08 07   5 4 3 2 1

Cover design by Borel Graphics
Text layout and design by Kim Foote

Text set in Goudy Old Style

ISBN 10: 0-88378-274-X
ISBN 13: 978-0-88378-274-3
Library of Congress Control Number: 2006908841

Artwork:
cover, p. 125: *Scarred* © by Melanie Henderson
p. 1: *digital the regal* © by Stephen Mead
p. 43: *dormi d'amore* © by Stephen Mead
p. 77: *Marlon, Wade in the Water* © by menoukha case

Contents

SECTION III
Pulsing Somewhere Distant

SECTION IV
We, the Meeting of Twin Edges, the Same Blood

Foreword: Why this Book?

Haki R. Madhubuti

Fingernails Across the Chalkboard is an answer to a question we, as Black people in this world, did not even know we were asking. The editors of this volume have long known the necessity of gathering voices that can speak frankly and honestly about HIV/AIDS and expect dialogue, argument and thoughtful exchange; and their questions are: not just "why?" but, "why not this book?" As I read each of the contributions in this anthology, I found myself reflecting on these questions and even my own body of work.

I write these words for people of all cultures, races, nationalities and religions. Having been intimately involved in Black and political struggle for all of my adult life, I remain a realistic optimist. Yet, as we quickly approach 2007, Blacks in the Diaspora, from Africa to India, from the Caribbean to the United States, are confronting the frailty of life itself. Too many, far too many of our young, and not so young, are fighting for their tomorrows as carriers of the HIV/AIDS virus. Most of them inhabit a cruel world of ignorant and angry accusers who do not care or understand the human damage that their words and inactions transmit.

In 1991, when I wrote my book *Black Men: Obsolete, Single and Dangerous?*, using current knowledge of the day, I attempted to confront the deadly and misunderstood questions of AIDS. At that time I, as did most informed observers, felt that this disease was a time bomb that had already exploded and was about to hit the Black world. I wrote:

> If there was one subject I was sure that I would not write about, it was AIDS (Acquired Immune Deficiency Syndrome). Like most misinformed, confirmed heterosexuals, I was convinced that AIDS was a white middle-class homosexual disease that, at worse, would only touch Black homosexuals. I also felt that the AIDS reports coming out of Afrika were exaggerated, and that white people were doing what they normally do with things that had gotten out of hand, *blame the victim*. As the saying goes, "ignorance is bliss." Well, in this case ignorance kills; and AIDS, unlike anything else that has invaded the Black World or any world, has the potential of devastating the Afrikan population unlike any weapon we've known since the Afrikan holocaust, the enslavement of Afrikan people by Europeans.

I read most of the available literature which included T.E. Bearden's *AIDS: Biological Warfare* (1980), William Campbell's *AIDS: The End of Civilization* (1989), papers published by the Panos Institute, "AIDS and the Third World" (1989), and from *Health Consciousness* "Who Murdered Africa" (1989) by William C.

Douglass, and much more. However, it was a friend who had confronted AIDS, and whose story I share in *Black Men*, that brought the human cost directly close to home:

> Max Robinson, a friend and brother in struggle, the first African American news anchor on national network television, became very ill and was isolated in a hospital outside of Chicago. Upon seeing him, I was inwardly crushed by his loss of weight and his emaciated look. It was difficult to keep the tears back. However, Max did not tell me that he had AIDS, and he was in good spirits; according to him, he was improving quickly and would be able to go home soon. I let it go at that, and two months later—without my seeing him again—Max was dead. It was his wish that people know he died of AIDS and that he did not contract it through the *assumed avenues* of drug use or homosexual activity. Max was a woman's man to the bone (one of his problems), and he did drink a great deal. However, he wanted his death to mean something and hoped that his community would begin to respond more positively to the current crisis. He knew that the topic of AIDS was such a taboo in the African American world that even he, as strong as he was, could only share it with a few family members and trusted friends.

The language of illness is too often the language of neglect, arrogance, superiority and blame. The act of putting the "other" in the closet or on crowded corners where help or hope has all but disappeared. Among the misinformed, their desire is that the infected be quiet, or better yet suffocate in painful silence. We are now surrounded by the powerfully *pure*, the know-it-all folks, bathing in a culture of religious righteousness and enlightenment, whose next life is defined as one free of the "riff-raff" who cannot control their libido's or addictions.

Medical ignorance is the norm in this country, where much of the information that is transmitted is beamed from AM and FM talk-radio, with political agendas that are draped in fear and cultural shallowness.

Accurate knowledge of HIV/AIDS is still almost non-existent, especially among the "end of days" folk who feel that those men and women who do not think, look or feel about the world as they do, are somehow incapable of enlightened discourse.

So again, we ask, Why this book? We publish *Fingernails Across the Chalkboard: Poetry and Prose on HIV/AIDS from the Black Diaspora* to directly counter the waves of misinformation that swims freely, almost never confronted in the Black world. This must stop. This is our contribution to intelligent discussion on the subject.

Haki R. Madhubuti
Poet,
Distinguished University Professor,
Professor of English and Director of the Master of Fine Arts in Creative Writing at Chicago State University,
Publisher of Third World Press

Introduction

Randall Horton, M. L. Hunter, and Becky Thompson

For twenty-five years, confronting AIDS, particularly in communities of color, has been like listening to fingernails across the chalkboard—sending chills down our spines, encouraging people to cover their ears. This volume encourages us to be willing to hear the sounds—the cries and anger—knowing that embodied in that rage is a history of struggle and survival. The writers and artists in this anthology tell us that we need to record HIV in a way that humanizes it and celebrates the living. All of the writers, in one way or another, are teaching us that beauty lives in the ugly: in the terribly beautiful.

To our knowledge, *Fingernails Across the Chalkboard* is the first anthology to offer literary perspectives on HIV among people of African descent in both the United States and Africa. The authors in this volume hail from Nigeria, the Netherlands, England, South Africa, and the United States. They include seasoned writers as well as many who are beginning to make a name for themselves within the architecture of literature. They are the next generation that will define the dialogue in the years to come. Many of them write experimental poetry and prose, taking many risks. They put everything on the table, refusing to hold back.

When AIDS was first officially recognized in 1981, it was portrayed as a white gay man's disease, a curse from God, and a death sentence. Dr. Ho, *Time* magazine's man of the year in 1996, along with many other researchers, gave the world the gift of a cocktail therapy that removed the death sentence for those who could afford these drugs. Shortly after this scientific breakthrough, HIV/AIDS moved from front-page news stories to snippets typically sprinkled on the media's back pages. The days of Ryan White and other stories of HIV/AIDS were gone. In the meantime, the long-term international consequences of the cocktail have yet to be determined.

During the twenty-five-year course of the disease, race, class, and gender inequities have crippled access to quality health care for millions of people. At the same time, much has yet to be written about HIV, particularly the impact of the disease on people across the African Diaspora. As Truth Thomas teaches in his prose poem in this volume, "although they comprise only 10% of the world's population, Africans constitute more than 60% of the AIDS-infected population... Although they comprise only 12% of the US population, African Americans constitute 50% of the AIDS infected population."

When Nelson Mandela was released from prison in 1990, he spoke in Boston and New York City about an umbilical cord that has long existed between South Africa and people of African descent in the United States. The disproportionate number of black people with HIV in Africa and the Western hemisphere is a 21st century version of that cord, reminding us that the future of black people in the world depends upon recognizing our linked histories and yearnings for freedom.

The emergence of this anthology has a layered history. It begins with co-editor M. L. Hunter's national call in 2004 for writing dealing with HIV in communities of color. During the previous year, the 14th Gwendolyn Brooks Black Writers' Conference in Chicago had sponsored a Positive Poetry Slam, making it the first major writer's conference in the United States to explicitly focus on HIV/AIDS. That same year, the HIV Youth Prevention Program in Chicago expanded its conference to encourage writers to creatively include HIV in their work. Hunter's initial call for writing did not bring in nearly enough submissions, a reality that reflects a history of fear, silence and avoidance of the issue. With the encouragement of poet Quraysh Ali Lansana, Director of the Gwendolyn Brooks Center for Black Literature and Creative Writing, Hunter teamed up with Randall Horton at Chicago State University, where both were graduate students in the MFA in Creative Writing program.

Aware of the urgent need to write about the impact of HIV on Black people across the Diaspora, and the continued barriers to such writing, Hunter and Randall knew that they would have to dig deep to find submissions that were of the quality and depth they envisioned. Along the way, they pulled in our third editor, Becky Thompson, because they wished to add a woman's voice to the mix. Becky had been working on HIV-related issues during the early years and knew about the disease's twenty-five year span.

We issued more than 100 calls for submissions, contacted many people directly, and postponed more than one deadline in the process. The three of us knew that although previous writing on HIV had been powerful historically, the pandemic, transnational character of HIV was calling for new voices, new perspectives. From the responses we received to our submission calls from writers worldwide, we learned that writing about HIV in communities of color does exist. We stand in awe of the quality, guts, and honesty of writing that follows this Introduction.

We have each brought a particular history, politics, and motivation to the project, which we shared with each other as we worked together. In one of her poems included in this volume,

Arisa White writes: "...I see you/with your lips stitched hesitant to speak of how someone you/knew got infected." As editors, we have decided to open this volume with our own unstitching: one particular, interconnected story at a time.

M. L. Hunter

Fingernails Across the Chalkboard *has been a long time coming for me. My early motivation for working in the HIV field was financial gains. At that time, I had no passion; I aimlessly existed. I was unconsciously dealing with who I was, how I wanted to be a productive individual, and how I fit in this world. I escaped by reading Marlon Riggs, Joseph Beam, and Essex Hemphill, who were fighting for black gay men.*[1] *They were also advocating for people with HIV. I was able to find a connection in their works to my life. I have always had a strong relationship to African American literature, especially poetry, but now I was reading insightful materials that reflected my existence.*

Umar Hasan, one of my first close friends when I was in college, was one of the first people I knew living with HIV. Umar was a poet writing with a zeal and energy I could feel in the work of Marlon, Joseph, and Essex as well. Umar wrote, among other lines, "brick walls don't give love," in a poem about his father. In another poem, "The Day Hurricane Elisa Hit Home," he wrote:

> I had these little red shorts,
> if you ain't got the looks use what works,
> and they worked.
> I'd run during rush hour
> so all my neighbors would see me
> sometimes they even yelled
> "Yooohooo, child, I want to drink your sweat."
> I would hit them with a rainstopping come back

"Hey, if you can keep up, I'll let you bottle it."

...

But, now my sweat isn't as sweet and

walking two blocks brings about thunderous coughs.[2]

The speaker takes readers on the journey from being able to run five miles before becoming HIV positive to barely being able to walk two city blocks.

During The Children's Hour in 1989, one of the first black gay pride celebrations in the United States, I visited Umar, who left Indiana University after my first year there (1986-87) to complete his degree at Howard University. That was my introduction to "the life." Umar became more of a brother to me from that point as I learned about black gay life. Wherever I was—in Washington, DC, or in Indianapolis, where Umar was— he and I did poetry slams together. I lost to him all the time but we kept slamming. He kept teaching me to love and empower myself. Unknowingly, I was collecting tools. Umar was my Essex Hemphill, my Marlon Riggs.

I still remember one of our phone conversations in the spring of 1994 when he first told me that the world (including me) would be losing him. During that conversation, I was encouraging him to get his Master's degree, but Umar told me that he wouldn't be around in six months. It hit me that he was telling the truth. I felt scared. I realized that one day, he might not be here. I had actually grown up down the highway from Ryan White, but I wasn't seeing HIV as others were. The only death I had experienced of someone significant in my life was my friend Patricia Griest, who had died five years earlier to lupus. I had never lost someone to AIDS. That night after our phone call, all I knew to do was write a poem, with the premise that tears have never answered prayers:

If a heart could cry a tear
I'd drench your soul to keep it near
feelings of forgiveness make me wanna cry
I hate to say it brother
I thought what was going to happen to me once you die.

"Letters" became the working title for the piece. It was a letter to Umar and Patricia, who also had left me tools for life. The poem was also about making letters: words and sound to give voice to my loss. I sent Umar a copy of the poem in calligraphy, and he gave me his approval and praise. I was beginning to feel my passion for working in the battle against HIV/AIDS.

Through the months, Umar and I kept talking. He told me that he couldn't afford AZT. Although he was working for a university outside of DC, he was struggling financially. Umar drank heavily, and I felt he was throwing his life away. He wanted to be in love. He wanted to be successful. And at the end of his life, I saw Umar wanting to live. When he was dying, he made some phone calls. He got some people's answering machines. People heard a ghostly voice. He said that at his funeral, he wanted people to know he died of complications from AIDS.

When I got a call from his brother that Umar had passed, we drove to DC the next morning. In the absence of his father, who could not accept his son's sexuality, and the presence of his mother, who did not know all that her son faced in his life, Umar was given the proper Muslim funeral at the hands of his brothers. During the reception in his apartment, I saw the card I sent him with the poem. I felt a sense of approval.

At the time of Umar's death I was in my first professional position working with HIV issues in Indiana. After a couple of years with the health department, I was hired as the Director of Camp Tataya Mato (meaning "breath of the bear"), Indiana's first camp for children and their families living with HIV/AIDS. My job was to get the camp started in Indianapolis. This meant raising money and awareness to make the camp a reality. I met families and numerous individuals who were prepared to join in this effort. Among those who came to the camp was a white woman from Bloomington, who had adopted two African American children, a girl and a boy, both of whom were born HIV-positive. While visiting their home to invite them to the camp, the little girl wanted to write her name for me. She was all of five years old at the time, living with HIV and quite aware. Her innocence was protecting her childhood. I looked at her as she ran around enjoying life and *writing her name for me, with some of her letters backwards. She and all the children I worked with for the next two years became my heroes because they were living.*

By the time I left Indianapolis for Chicago in 1997, I was ready to start living my life. Chronologically, I was turning 30; emotionally, I was a newborn. I had to introduce myself to myself and I was scared. Nothing could save me, but I was beginning to recognize and try to use tools left by Umar and Patricia. I had my memories of the heroes from Tataya Mato. I had my experience working with the health department. And I had my love of poetry. I had been introduced to poetry early in life: Gwendolyn Brooks, Langston Hughes, Maya Angelou. Just thinking about poets thrilled me, and still does. This love, along with my experiences surrounding HIV during the 1990s to the present day, has nourished my passion. For years, I had no idea how to handle my power. As I have been growing into myself, I have been prepared by the universe to contribute to Fingernails Across the Chalkboard.

Randall Horton

Working on this anthology marks my first bold step in confronting HIV/AIDS, a controversial political issue I have always put on the back burner. As I have come into my own as a poet, I've realized that I have to face the realities I fear most. Having been on the streets for many years, dealing with prostitutes and drug dealers, I saw HIV and its repercussions all the time, but I never thought I might get infected.

Denial is how I dealt with HIV. At the beginning, I thought of HIV as a gay disease but I soon saw differently. I knew a woman named Tracy who was a prostitute. Her daily job was to turn as many tricks as she could in order to buy enough cocaine for her habit. I knew she was positive. I also knew she was engaging in unprotected sex. But I felt a connection to her, because everybody else had dogged her out. I tried to be sure she always had something to eat, a place to stay. But I was in total denial about her being sick or infecting other people. This was a silent dialogue between Tracy and me; words were never spoken. She was nothing but bones, all dressed up, working every day to get a date. Her addiction would not let her sit still. I erased from my thoughts that she might die. I only wanted to see her live. But I denied her the simple humanity of being a person first, by not even talking about it or giving her encouragement. I will never forget her. She is probably dead now.

I was living a life where HIV was everywhere, but still, I decided to turn my back. When I first went to prison, I had no awareness, period. In prison, seeing guys who were HIV positive made me think about the risks I had taken. It scared me. I escaped HIV through dumb luck. I was walking around with a .45 pointed to my head, squeezing the trigger every few minutes. Guys who are HIV positive in prison taught me that in spite of it all, you gotta keep living. They are dealing with HIV and many other issues. Each person accepts his lot and moves on. They didn't look at it as a death sentence; instead, it was, "if you get it, you deal with it, and you live." When I was in a drug program for two years (part of my prison sentence) I met a teenager who had sold her body to men for drugs for most of her life. After the drug program, she got her life together. She decided she was not going to let her positive status determine her position in the world. She is going to college now, getting her degree, working in banking, and looking and loving toward the future. We have remained close.

In the process of working on this anthology, HIV has ceased to scare me like it used to. I have seen that people are living. They are working. I have also learned more about how people contract it, including children who are raped and become infected. When I was reading the submissions for the book, I found myself gravitating toward the writing that dealt with child abuse—in church settings, in families, and on the street. I have come to believe that you can't talk about the subject of child abuse enough. It is uncertain how many people have been infected through abuse. We do know that the people who transmit HIV to children often know they are infected.

In Arisa White's poem, which is written to a child, the narrator asks hard questions and gives hard answers about life, about getting infected, about being abused. "So young pretty you are so tight you are virgin mythologized/left broken to cup the spilling of a positive penis, from your/ edges comes no cure, you meet your adolescence with AIDS."

Like White, Dwayne Betts writes from the point of view of someone whose story has largely been ignored. In this case, it is the mother of a girlfriend seeing a man after he has returned from prison. "Your Mother's Questions" deals with men in prison who have sex with each other, a common occurrence. The mother in the poem knows when men get out, they don't necessarily tell their partners the truth, compromising their partner's trust and health. While the mother wants to protect her daughter, the man being questioned is, rightfully, wary of the stereotypes and interrogation aimed in his direction.

Evie Shockley's poem, "A Question of Survival," asks, "are we defined/by what we/can survive or/what we can't?" This forces us to consider if the use of experimental drugs is turning people into guinea pigs and consider if drug trials are more about exploiting people for money than for saving people's lives.

Melanie Henderson raises another ethical issue with her words. In asking, "[are you] only human if your body is/a self sufficient, self healing/ war machine," she challenges us to rethink the notion that humanity is rated by one's ability to regenerate oneself.

Like Henderson, Dike Okoro ponders about what the living need to know. He writes, "Today I stand over your mound/not mad at you for what you did not teach us/but at myself for failing/to drag you to the river/when I knew its knowledge ran in my veins." The knowledge that Okoro speaks of is essential for combating HIV/AIDS in the 21st century. Also in regards to taking action, avery r. young writes, "condoms do more than keep stains off dresses." He reminds us that safe sex (and likewise, humor) remains a must.

The writers offer us much knowledge to digest. As a whole, the volume teaches us that the last chapter of HIV has yet to be written. The writers leave us with the following question: what will we do to make an ending possible?

Becky Thompson

When I attended the first annual AIDS conference in Denver in 1983, many people were still calling it GRID (Gay Related Immune Deficiency). People in San Francisco were still getting off busses on certain city streets, thinking that they might get infected through the air they were breathing. What I still remember about the Denver conference, almost a quarter of a century later, are the gay men who took over a table full of microphones at one of the plenary sessions. They did so because they realized they knew more at that point about AIDS than the doctors did. It was up to them to seize the time, to share as much knowledge with each other as they could, to advocate into each other's arms. Feminists, both lesbian and straight, were right there with them, teaching the men what women had already learned–that patient-centered health care would demand that men take charge of their own health. The men needed to "our bodies, ourselves" their way into safe sex, peer-led education programs, and community health programs. At that point, however, while white gay men were doing much to save their own lives, as important as this work was, those being blamed for the disease were being separated into camps: white gay men in one, Haitians in another, people using drugs in another, prostitutes in another, hemophiliacs in yet another. As President Reagan practiced an unconscionable policy of silence and denial, people with HIV had to fend for themselves. Both in the United States and across the globe, those with resources–money, white skin privilege, citizenship rights, and insurance–fared much better than everybody else.

When Joseph Beam, Marlon Riggs, Essex Hemphill, Issac Julian, and other black gay men started writing, filming, and publishing their work in the 1980s, the earth turned on its axis.[3] They started to break down the deadly divides between people who desperately needed to work together. In his introduction to Hemphill's second book, Ceremonies, critic and scholar Charles Nero drew a parallel between the historical silence about the Middle Passage and silence about HIV in the black community.[4] Nero linked Toni

Morrison's dedication of *Beloved* to "*the sixty million and more who endured, suffered and died during this Holocaust*" to Essex Hemphill's work—his brave and creative commitment to writing as a black gay man who was HIV positive. In one of his most well-known poems, "When My Brother Fell," dedicated to Black gay writer and activist Joseph Beam, Hemphill wrote that when Beam died after compiling the first anthology of black gay writing in US history, "I picked up his weapons and never once questioned/whether I could carry the weight and grief...He had fallen/and the passing ceremonies/marking his death/did not stop the war."

Hemphill had picked up the work Beam had begun, and everybody around him knew it. Beam, Hemphill, Riggs, Julian, and other black gay men knew from their own experiences, what Cherríe Moraga and Gloria Anzaldúa meant when they titled their foundational anthology: This Bridge Called My Back.[5] Indeed, these black gay men bridged work between men in choir boxes and men in leather on San Francisco's Castro Street, as well as between their mothers, fathers, and grandparents; between the CDC and community health clinics; and between gay organizers in South Africa and Act UP in the United States. In his last public appearance before he died in 1995, Hemphill read poems for an enraptured audience at the historic Black Nations? Queer Nations? Conference in New York City. Essex had everybody laughing when he said that he knew everybody wants to think they descended from kings and queens in Africa, but someone had to carry the water and clean the pyramids. He had everyone crying when he admitted that had he known years ago the kind of love he was experiencing now, he would have walked out of the bathhouses immediately. He said, "I stand here, counting T cells in cyberspace." My respect for Essex—his beauty, honesty, vulnerability, and brave poetry—is why I wanted to work on this volume.

HIV Positive

Because of our different historical connections to HIV activism, Hunter and Becky almost had a fight—actually, more like an animated discussion—when Hunter said he didn't want the volume to focus on gay men of color. Becky argued for keeping sexuality, including homosexuality, in the equation no matter what. This would include same-sex relationships in prison, which are still not openly acknowledged; women getting HIV from partners who do not admit their homosexuality; and young gay men who think that because of the cocktail, HIV is no big deal. Hunter opposed. Based on his many years working in public health, he expressed that in 2006, people still think of HIV as a "gay thing." He argued that we as a society have to move beyond this perception, considering that far less gets publicized about HIV's impact on other populations, such as straight mothers, straight men, and religious people. He reasoned that though there has been important recent work on down low culture (*The New York Times* exposé, Keith Boykin's widely read book), little is available about how to empower straight women dealing with such men.[6]

Our argument led to a shared vision: a hope to compile an anthology that could speak to both the church folks and to the flamboyant queens. We also wanted it to resonate with adolescents infected HIV, as well as with the man just released from prison who wants to do right in an intimate relationship. In taking this initiative, *Fingernails Across the Chalkboard* will follow in the tradition of collections by Joseph Beam, Umar Hasan, and Essex Hemphill. We hope that it can carry the torch of AIDS/HIV activism and awareness, spearheaded by those such as Noerrine Kaleeba of Uganda, who became an internationally known activist after her husband died from AIDS complications; and Nelson Mandela, who wore a t-shirt reading, "HIV Positive," and offered up his son's T cell count as he helped to move the Mbeki administration to deal effectively with the epidemic in South Africa.[7] Our hope was for a volume that could keep issues on sexuality and gay men present but would not feed into old stereotypes of HIV as a "gay thing"; a volume that comes from the US but does not repeat the myopic internal gaze so prevalent in AIDS work through the 1990s.

We have loosely organized the writing into four interconnected sections. "Stop Walking for a Minute, Hear Me"[8] addresses hard-hitting truths surrounding HIV/AIDS: how people are first introduced to it in their lives, how they learn that their loved ones are positive, and how they decide to speak openly about their status. "So Young Pretty"[9] confronts multiple forms of abuse surrounding HIV: incest and rape in the lives of girls and women, which leaves them especially vulnerable to becoming infected; violations of trust, due to infidelity in relationships; corporate abuse, by pharmaceutical companies, of people who desperately need humane care. "Pulsing Somewhere Distant"[10] addresses grieving and loss (in other words, the "life for me ain't been no crystal stair" part of the anthology). The authors in this section consider what grief feels like when, as Ifeayni Ajeabo writes, "outside, the sound of the night has stopped." "We, the Meeting of Twin Edges, the Same Blood," includes writing about rebelling and resisting, activism and justice. In the words of South African poet and activist Dennis Brutus, included here, we encourage everyone to "have festivals to challenge AIDS."

Essex Hemphill always signed the end of his letters with: "take care of your blessings—fiercely." We want to second that emotion. Italicize "*fiercely*."

Notes

1. Essex Hemphill, *Ceremonies* (San Francisco: Cleis Press, 1992); Essex Hemphill and Joseph Beam, ed., *Brother to Brother: New Writings by Black Gay Men* (Boston: Alyson, 1991); Joseph Beam, ed. *In the Life: A Black Gay Anthology* (Boston: Alyson, 1986).

2. Umar Hasan, *Milking Black Bull: Eleven Gay Black Poets*, conceived by Assotto Saint, edited by Vega (Sicklerville, New Jersey: Vega Press, 1995).

3. Films: Issac Julian, *Looking for Langston* (1989); Marlon Riggs, *Tongues Untied* (1989) and *Black Is/Black Ain't* (1995). Publications: Essex Hemphill, *Ceremonies* (ibid.); Essex Hemphill and Joseph Beam, ed., *Brother to Brother* (ibid.); Essex Hemphill, *Conditions* (New York: Be Bop Books, 1986); Joseph Beam, ed. *In the Life: A Black Gay Anthology* (ibid.).

4. Charles Nero, "Fixing Ceremonies: An Introduction," in Essex Hemphill, ed., *Ceremonies* (San Francisco: Cleis Press, 1992), xii.

5. Cherríe Moraga and Gloria Anzaldúa, eds. *This Bridge Called My Back: Writings By Radical Women of Color* (New York: Kitchen Table Women of Color Press, 1983).

6. Benoit Denizet-Lewis, "Double Lives on the Down Low," *The New York Times Magazine*, August 3, 2003: 28-33, 48, 52-53; Keith Boykin, *Beyond the Down Low: Sex, Lies, and Denial in Black America* (New York: Carroll & Graph, 2005).

7. "The Age of AIDS," *Frontline*, PBS. May 30, 2006.

8. Title from Sections I and IV from Arisa White's poem, "My Dead."

9. Title from Arisa White's poem, "Believe Them When They Say."

10. Title from Alan King's poem, "Scope."

SECTION I

Stop Walking for a Minute, Hear Me

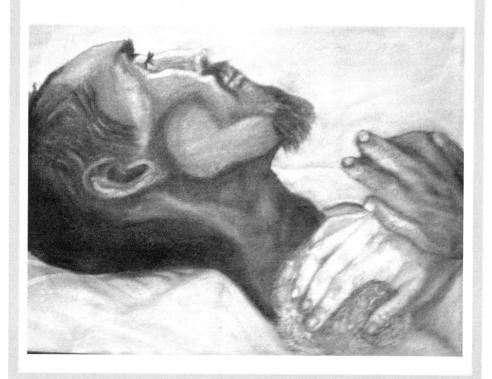

HIV/AIDS

Dennis Brutus

for Melvin Dixon, Guild Complex, and Street Beat

And now
better than ever before
in the history of the world
we understand
how the instruments of love
are the instruments of death
and how love
though it endures all things
must be handled
very delicately

November 10, 1995
Pittsburgh, PA

We Real Crunk

Frank X. Walker

after Gwendolyn Brooks

We Real Crunk. We
Buy junk. We

Walk slow. Wear
Pants low. We

Sling rocks. Run
From cops. We

Get laid. Die
From AIDS.

My Dead

Arisa White

She died everybody she died another is dead everybody
dead and AIDS everybody of AIDS she is my dead everybody
and I know there are more of you with the same story hiding
behind walls I see you from your windows I see you
with your lips stitched hesitant to speak of how someone you
knew got infected

old lady watching the neighborhood breathe you know
how we cast dirt on the dead long before they have reached
the ground you know how we shun those that don't die
of natural causes who lost themselves in dissolution
we give them our backs the unguarded susurrations:
she should she should she should have known better

to be sleeping with some shiftless recovering drug addict
she should she should she she should have known
who knows this when they have stripped down
to their most tender parts bodies posture welcome

who knows that when you disrobe you possibly
invite death she is my dead you on the corner

want to name me madwoman know that I anguish
in pieces over and over in my head I look to see her
take to the periphery her walk the click of dying bones
she ambient sounds she preparing us for her absence she
afraid to come around the family we could no longer match
her to the beauty we knew

everybody stop walking for a minute hear me
in this scream of cars she had genital warts the size
of her son's two year old fist she had them laser removed
she could not walk it hurt so bad it hurt to take a piss
so bad ached her thighs who would come into her to love

with both of my hands I alone step her from her clothes
undress myself and there I sit legs parted waiting for her
to fit her behind in the curve of my pelvic bone I
braid her hair part and grease her scalp weave it
into cornrows I breathe against the cliffs of her
shoulder blades my breast in the basin of her spine

we the meeting of twin edges the same blood we are people
from down South we got each other genealogy we are familiar
no need for introduction she is my dead in my arms my collar
her head rests reclines into me the tension that held her taut
falls to the sheets I am left holding her soft parts her breast
the mumble beneath her left nipple

her pussy the pit of cantaloupe when it has been sitting
on the counter all day she opens to my half prayer fits
me inside of her she moans that cantaloupe bursts its architecture

into pieces seeds stick to my wrists deep into the melon fingers
glisten darker shade in its juices she moans and I taste lick from each
my palms the runaway droplets from my arms who would love her

I taste the alchemy of sun water dirt I alone all the things
she ate the sea of lime the tart of sweet slick with my saliva
across my tongue alive between my lips her clit wakes the morning
at six she is my dead and to my side of the mattress her legs pedal
her body the sheets foldout of breath deflates beneath my touch
her absence heats the bed.

Autobiography Aid

Deborah Poe

for Paul Dees

As he crashed through my front door, a hovering.   As if
a best friend   expected speech. As if I expected him.   And in
this moment, none of that. No more than an arrival.   A coming.
A going. A room. A coma.
It was later that she came.

–

There was nothing in the room but language. A white gown like a
period, a sick room a comma, the edge of fainting   close to
moments ago a colon, her grief parenthetical.   As if
she wasn't sure I could hear, she spoke to me. My body in its
seventh day of coma, contextual, uncooperative, and unwavering.
And a room without windows. And uncomfortable friends
awkward in their leaving. At 50 pounds, I was striking. So she said.

–

Even these days in a coma, the connection came, a surprise.

Each day the heart heaved. *All the love in the world goes with you. Go
easy, but you go.**

—

I didn't take my medicine. I didn't say I'm sick. A contribution to
denial.   Capable of disassociating, from problems outside
of my control,   I don't think denial was dementia.   The
latter came late in my disease. I couldn't plant tomato plants.
          I perceived tomatoes also, outside my control.
The ten tomato plants.   My son's red hair.
Her red hair.   Red climbing trees.   de Maupassant.   *Timbuctoo*
and *Tombstones*.

—

Like everyone, I liked to sex. Valentine's should be celebrated.
Different than the Billie Holiday CD or the balloon with wine I
left her earlier, I laid her on her stomach,   pulled out
handcuffs. Everything in her shook un-cynical.   Surely I
must have been sick by then.

—

Watching a basketball game, I took gulps of weed. On huge floor
pillows. I noticed her watching. Watching my shoulders. The way I
stooped.   I'm two years older. I must have looked old. Yes I must
have looked old. But now I understand.   She
knew a year before the others.
                    She saw it in the body. She saw me dying before
I died.

* Mark Doty, from *Heaven's Coast*

Results

Tara Betts

Open envelopes
unleash death warrants
HIV positive.

Guatemalan Postscript

Ruth O'Callaghan

The shift of light burnishes the pan in her hand,
its faded "Made in Guatemala" sticker peels
back to paths where birds jabber bruises
her ears and his hand stops her mouth, leaving
his empty promise on the forest floor.

Confused, she dances for her lover, her matted
hair swaying as he re-fastens his belt, slashes
creepers from his path, laughs and spits, flicks
calloused fingers: in the quick spurt of dust
from his spurred heel, a used coin dies.

Now she forgets the pan searing her hand, hearing
the cotinga's screech behind the doctor's diagnosis,
seeing the sarcoma: her lover beckons,
she reaches through the pane
to soft earth fourteen floors below.

Thembi's Song

Tony Medina

when she was young her
pretty eyes lit up my sky
her smile was all mine
her face the first thing I saw
calming and warm like the sun

when she was young she
looked so old nothing but skin
and bones and sores and
scars and coughing and wheezing
like an old broken down car

when she was sick I
prayed she would get better
her face would fill up
with sun her eyes full of hope
and joy flowering again

Confronting My Mortality

Gerald Ribeiro

My experience living with the virus has been different in a lot of ways from those of many people. When I found out I had AIDS, my family came and stood by me. From the day I knew, they knew. I didn't hold onto the secret as some people do, where the secret becomes such a fear and burden it becomes bigger than life. I never experienced what many people with the virus have experienced, where even family members ostracize you. My nieces can't wait for Uncle Gerald to hold their babies.

Halloween is my anniversary. It always brings up deep emotions, survivor's guilt being one. I think that most people go through life denying death; most have that luxury where they don't think about it daily. But living with AIDS has put me in a position where I've had to deal with my mortality on a nose-to-nose, upfront-and-personal basis. Every day I'm steadily wrestling with that issue—both in my own life and in terms of people around me.

When I was first diagnosed, I bounced between denial and complete fear. There was no real middle ground. In the beginning, I didn't think about it every day, especially the first five years when I was still active in my addiction. I spent more time thinking about not feeling. I didn't deal with my mortality or what it would be like to be sick, to go through one of the crises so many people with AIDS face.

When I began to get one infection or another, hepatitis this or mono that, I was terrified because they originally told me I had a year or so to live. I remember beginning to get sick with an opportunistic infection, pneumocystic pneumonia, and then getting real sick and being in the hospital with a high temperature they couldn't get down. I was so afraid. When I finally left the hospital, I walked away with a sense of enlightenment, a feeling of accomplishment from going through this frightful experience. Up to that point, my perception was that the virus was not part of me, but something foreign that had invaded my body that I wanted to get out of me. Once I accepted that the virus—like my addiction—was part of the total sum of who I was and what my life experience was, I found a kind of peace.

When my infectious disease doctor first spoke to me about the protease inhibitors, he compared them to the insulin that diabetics take. That comparison revealed how much faith he had put in them and what they could do for people with the virus. I had gotten to the point where I had accepted the virus, accepted the fact I was not going to live a normal life in terms of my life span, and that death probably wasn't going to be pretty. I don't think any death is, but the vision I've always had of the virus and what it does to people over a period of time until they die: it's like taking a straw man and pulling him apart one straw at a time until there's nothing left.

I had a fear that if I bought into the hope about what the protease inhibitors were capable of doing, I would disrupt that place of acceptance I had found, especially if they didn't prove to be as successful as my doctor thought they would be. So I never allowed myself to totally believe in them. That skepticism ended up being lucky for me, because after a year or so of taking protease inhibitors, the doctors found out my body was resistant to them. I had to go back to the old family of AIDS drugs, the AZT group. I got on a regimen of AZT, 3TC, and a new drug at that time called Abacavir.

The medicines are doing a job that is beneficial for my long-term survival. But every day I'm sick in terms of nausea, stomach pains, body aches, temperatures every now and then, and feeling lethargic and tired. There may be some breaks along the way, where for several hours I feel pretty good, and I'm not thinking about how I'm feeling physically. But I constantly struggle with getting out of bed every morning, taking my medicines, and making myself eat since I have to take my pills with food, and then go to work.

I moved my office to my house to make it easier for me to work and take naps when I felt tired. But it was not that helpful. I canceled more meetings in one year than in my ten years before. I'm not in a real physical crisis, but every day I feel the same way—tired, lethargic, weak, and nauseated. It wears on me on a physical, emotional, and mental level.

Sometimes I can push the virus and what it's doing to me out of my mind and focus on my work. When I go to meetings outside of the house, people look at me and sometimes say, "You look good." Because I'm at the meeting and participating, their subjective view is that Gerald's doing good. But my wife who sits with me and goes through it with me, she knows how much energy it takes for me to get to that place.

There's no getting used to waking up every day knowing your day's going to be miserable because of how you're feeling physically, which then affects you emotionally, which then affects you mentally. I sometimes feel like a dog chasing his tail. The cycle gets more intense, more difficult as I go along. Sometimes I get frustrated enough that I just want to throw up my hands and quit. I cannot picture being able to continue without having this compass that's pointing me in this direction where I'm saying to myself: "Your purpose is this and this is what you need to do," and then having the strength to follow through on that.

It helps me to understand what I'm fighting for, to understand there are external forces that put people in this position where they have to experience so much pain and hardship in their lives. That understanding is what pushes me; that's what carries me when I'm doing work I don't really have the strength to do.

Sometimes I wholeheartedly believe in the work that I'm doing, that we human beings on this planet need to take responsibility to make change, to struggle against every kind of oppression. Then there are other times I wonder if I'm struggling with my own demons and this is how I deal with it. I'm trying to right the wrongs I've done. Dealing with this *tick-tick-tick-tick* I hear in my head, I wonder how much time I've got left. It's a wonder I always live with. Sometimes this lack of certainty pushes me to do more than I had in the past or to take on more issues than I probably should. One of the lessons this disease has taught me, and it's always teaching me lessons, is I need to have more of a balance.

When my oldest daughter, Nsenga, was in nursing school, she had an assignment to talk to someone who was dealing with a chronic or terminal illness. At the end of her phone interview with me, I told her I felt the virus was a gift. She got quiet. I said, "What's the matter?" She replied, "I don't understand how you can say that. My father probably won't be here to see my kids grow up. Why would you say that?" She seemed perplexed, but I could also hear an edge of anger in her voice.

I explained to her I saw it as a gift because it put passion in my life. "If someone came to you and said, I give you a gift and it's a gift of passion, which means that everything you do in life you will do to the best of your ability, then you will always be in the moment. If you were cooking a meal, you would cook the best meal you could cook. If you were in school studying, you would study to the best of your ability. If you were listening to jazz, you would be in that moment and love the notes you were hearing. You would just really soak life in. If someone could offer you that gift, would you take it?" She answered, "Yeah, of course I would." I said, "Well, that's sort of what the virus has done for me."

But it's not a gift you go out and seek. Although I still believe it has helped me in many ways, I don't put the same value on that gift as I did back then. When I talk about it being a gift, that gift should be given in other ways, not by getting a life-threatening disease. That was me the martyr talking at that time. I don't feel so much like a martyr today because I love myself more today than I did then.

There's nothing much I can do about the situation, so I have to take what I've got and make it into a positive. No experience is completely negative if you learn from it. I believe the down periods in our lives are times when we're supposed to learn our most profound lessons. When I look at it in that sense, I say that when I come through this, I'm going to be an even stronger person with a much greater understanding.

You can try to deny death, but the medicines are a constant reminder of what you're dealing with. You know these handful of pills you're taking are doing damage along with good. In this instant gratification society we live in, when you take medicine, you like to see a quick response: you get a headache, you take an aspirin and the headache goes away. Even when it came to the illegal drugs: you're feeling depressed, you take the drug, the depression goes away. You take the AIDS drugs, but you don't know what they're doing to your system in terms of being effective or not.

I know other people who are long-term survivors, who are dealing with this disease like I am, who talk about the frustration of taking their pills every day and the frustration of feeling sick every day. I've seen people who couldn't do it, won't do it, who've said, "I'm not taking any more pills. Life's going to take its course with me." I can see why people give up, because every day is a constant battle. People give up because of the frustration of taking these medicines and not seeing any short-term and, in many cases, long-term change.

Every three months or so I get blood work to test the viral load and find out if my body, along with the medicines, is winning the struggle or not. Most of the time I come away feeling numb. Sometimes it's good news, which means that nothing has changed and the overall long-term prognosis is the same. My wife Shelly is more likely to focus on the positive aspects of what we hear from the doctor than I am.

Most nights when I'm taking out my medicine bag, setting all the pill bottles in front of me, then putting the pills into the daily pill container, it's a major letdown for me. Sometimes I try to get into a place where I'm not even focusing on what I'm doing and try to act like it ain't nothing. Other times the evening ritual is so frustrating that to get through it, I could be yelling and throwing the pills in the bag; it definitely changes the mood of the house at that moment.

I learned the importance of being compliant early on in the process of taking these AIDS drugs. When I first started taking them, no one explained to me the importance of not missing doses. Pills I was supposed to take three times a day I would sometimes take twice a day. Because my compliance at that point was probably around seventy, eighty percent, the virus mutated around them, and those drugs that would have probably worked in me longer, didn't work anymore.

Again, I have this fear about how I am going to get through this. When that question comes up, I say to myself, "you've been through this before, you can go through it again." I also have a lot of resources in terms of friends I can depend on, including friends who are in the business of dealing with people who are addicts. For me, it's invaluable to have people around me who can empathize with me but yet not be so caught up that it beats them down. They have the strength to say, "Hey, you gotta do this, hey, you gotta take this test.

Yes, I know the test is invasive. Yes, I know it's painful. But I'll be there with you."

Because of the virus itself and the heavy-duty medicines I take, my common bile duct was damaged. As a recovering addict the question I always wrestle with is, am I taking medication because I want to feel good or because I want to feel better? *Feel good*, meaning do I want a buzz? *Feel better*, do I want to take away my pain? I think it's been both, and there are times it's been either one or the other. This makes me feel anxious. Also, taking heavy doses of pain medicines incapacitates me to the point where sometimes I can do little or no work. This reality brings me back to that period where I was dependent on drugs. The fear of not being able to get it because the doctor might think you don't need it anymore, a sense of panic, to being locked up and those people who lock you up, for one reason or another, don't get you the medication. Just to be dependent in that way makes me feel almost like a victim. This is the issue I talk about with my doctors all the time, in terms of understanding why I'm on this medication and when am I going to get off it.

There have been times when we were talking about a medicine when the doctor said, "If and when you decide to get off this medicine..." I'm not sure what that means and I'm almost afraid to ask. I'm not sure if she thinks this will never be resolved in terms of the pain or if she thinks that for some reason it's not worth going through the pain and the process of getting off the medicine. Sometimes I feel like just rolling up my sleeves and saying, "Let's get this over with." That is the impatient part of me, the part of me that, when I think something is inevitable, I just want to get it over with.

That mentality has gotten me into trouble in the past. When I tried one time to get off a high dose of methadone in a two-week period, I went through a lot of pain and cried to get back on it. Because of the rules of the program, I had to wait a month. So I struggle to maintain the thought process, "You had to be on it, now it's time to get off it. Let's take the right steps so it doesn't set you up to do the wrong thing."

I think about a friend, a recovering addict living with the virus, a community leader in Boston, who just before he died, was active again in his drug use. I wonder where he was at mentally? Was he in the same place I'm at right now? Was he on pain medicine? Could he not get off it? Did he rush the process of getting off it? Did his doctors just cut him off of the pain medicines, making him think that his only option was to go to the street? Did he not have a strong, intimate support system around him? Did he lose his sense of purpose in life?

You Made Me Come Home

Dike Okoro

for Ebenezer (1968-2005)

I remember very well
Our talks under the mango tree
In moonlit nights
When you left us starving
For more of your storied
Legend with the city girls
What boys do to cover up
For the mysteries of manhood
You covered our fears
With your pleasure talks
Not the inroads to avoid the killer's tracks
You told us of the heights climbed
Between the legs of a woman
Not the ocean swallowing today
Our daughters and sons
Today I stand over your mound
Not mad at you for what you did not teach us
But at myself for failing

To drag you to the river
When I knew its knowledge ran in my veins

I read your last cry
In your mother's eyes yesterday
Watched her stumble
Between speech that refused to let out
When you were lowered
By the pallbearers
Ah, the betrayal of the times
Where parents are left
To bury their children
And the question of who will bury the old
Stabs the heart
Brother, you tried
Even when the doctor
Told you how many days you had left
You did not abandon your wife
And daughter
The two responsibilities you left
For those you loved to cater for
So much for words now
When the killer of tomorrow is still on rampage
And our youths are bread crumbs
On the table of the dreaded monster

normal

avery r. young

inside bathroom
swallow pills 42 to 21.
question why jee-sus
dont like dykes?

are we strange

visions of normal blastin
from idiot box interruptin
phil-busters of politicians caught
with their pants down?

note: condoms do more than keep stains off dresses.

Don't Ask, Just Know

Tara Betts

A declaration of a friend's bright blonde afro
the night of the family Christmas party
meant an awkward holiday—a pair of stiff jaws
wedged into silence between father and son.

I told the son, my friend that I always knew
his outing an obvious secret bubbling beneath
the skin, waiting to boil.

He called me for escapades with house music
and Janet Jackson bending blackened
warehouse walls of The Generator.

Sweating and red on the dance floor
without meat hooks aimed at my skin,
except for one woman I ducked
into a room swole with men in work boots.

Carhartts, overalls without shirts.
We gathered a crew in the cold.

Golden Nugget Pancake House
in all its diner grease glamour
was the final stop before families
reclaimed us in the sweep
of a New Year. We ordered
our starches of choice.

Under the dim lights, checked
our silverware, but the only spot
I noticed was a dark brown scab

the size of a pinky nail
balanced on one eyebrow.
I already knew not to ask.

The Memorial

Randi Triant

At eleven thirty at night, Logan Airport is as unwelcoming as a hospital: the lights are too bright and someone is being paged repeatedly over the PA system. My luggage has already arrived, but Monica hasn't. I consider sneaking out to a cab to delay seeing her even further.

I've come to Boston because the only man I've ever loved, Dean Johnson, made me promise I would. Before he died from AIDS, Dean made me swear that I'd co-host his memorial in Boston with the love of his life—Monica. The thing is Monica isn't a Monica. Monica is a man, a black man, which apparently is what mattered to Dean. Me, a white woman, I never got him within twenty feet of the bedroom. Not that I didn't try.

I rush through the revolving doors. There are only two people in the taxi line. No Monica. A serious-looking man is dutifully pointing us to our respective cabs, though there are at least ten yellow, beat-up sedans lined up. Why does he bother? I don't actually say that to him. Although I've lived in New York City for a year, it isn't a natural fit; I don't have that New Yorker honesty down yet. I wish I could be more like those people I see everyday, barking at the waiter that the bread is stale, muttering at someone who's holding up the line at the Post Office, loudly criticizing a bad theater performance. But I'm not. New York was an escape hatch, nothing more. A way out from Dean and Monica. I'd spent far too many nights with them at the Brattle watching film noir movies, Dean's favorite, or dining in cozy restaurants in the South End, night after night seeing Monica succeed where I hadn't, as Dean and I remained what we'd always been, best friends.

Mr. Taxi Pointer gives me the full up and down. It took me years to get over the fact that I was no longer that gangly, coke bottle-glassed geek I'd been in sixth grade. I still can't see myself as others do, as a tall and striking blond with contact enhanced blue eyes, who belongs in some country where they sip glogg. I start giving Mr. Taxi Pointer the once over right back at him. You're in bad shape when you start to ogle the taxi guy who's a foot shorter than you are and has the earmarks of being out in the cold too long: cement-colored cheeks and a red, dripping nose. Maybe it's because I haven't slept with anyone in months, not since I made the rather unfortunate mistake of picking up a partner at our firm's cocktail party honoring summer associates. Maybe it's what Dean called "the grief factor." After Dean watched so many of his friends die, he used to say that death makes you want to latch onto the nearest breathing thing. Maybe that's what's going on here, I am in town for Dean's memorial after all, but I can't give it much thought because I'm about to make a clean get-away, free of Monica.

In seconds, my suitcase is safely stowed in a cab's trunk and the cab pulls out but then there's a loud bang from the rear. I haven't slipped away fast enough. Monica is running behind the cab, hand outstretched ready to pound on the trunk again. "Stop! Carolyn! Stop!" she shouts through the back window.

The cab driver screeches the cab to a halt and pops the trunk from inside. No way he's getting out of the car to help me; he's undoubtedly frightened by the sight of Monica, a six foot-four man, with a blond shoulder-length wig, dressed in a tube top and red leather skirt, opening up my door.

"Thank God, I caught you," Monica says, smiling.

"There's a snag in the plans," she says before we've driven out of the parking lot. "The Lady of Our Once Beloved wants a thousand dollars."

"That's ridiculous," I tell her. "Besides, I don't think an accredited church would have a name like that, would they?" What I'm really thinking is, *are you out of your goddamn mind?*

"Oh, well, *accredited*. You public school girls have quite the vocab, don't you?"

This is a crack about my having gone to U. Mass. at Amherst. Monica never went to college; she graduated from beauty school and works on *chichi* Newbury Street. But five years of living with Dean, the Harvard graduate, gives her social standing a lift by osmosis. Before I can ask her how many heads she washed this week, Monica says, "The church isn't really called *that*. Look, I'll pay the thousand as soon as I can get into his bank accounts after the estate is settled. Just lend it to me for now."

I feel the vodka I drank on the plane reflux up the back of my throat. I've known for months that Dean wasn't leaving his estate to me but it still rankles. It was the least he could have done; Monica got *him* for five years. I hear Dean's voice, though, saying, "You should be nicer to her. You're everything she wants to be, Carolyn — you're a straight, beautiful woman."

"I'll lend you the money," I say.

"I really appreciate it," says Monica. I'm not doing it for *her*. I'm doing it for Dean. I couldn't care less what Monica appreciates. "The only other sticking point is his parents," Monica goes on.

"Are *they* coming?" Dean's parents are devout Catholics and spent most of Dean's adult life urging him to renounce his sinful ways and to come back home to the farm.

"Just to make our lives miserable. They called and the whole time they talked to me like I was just Dean's friend—someone he met through the Hasty Pudding Club, some place I wouldn't shouldn't couldn't show my face in."

By now we're through the Callahan Tunnel and merging into 93-South traffic. "That can't be right. He told them, I'm sure of it," I say to placate her. When Monica gets revved up, you never know what the outcome will be. It's better to put road blocks up early in the day.

"I know he told them, but they're pretending like he *didn't* tell them."

"Number 8," I say automatically and Monica lets out one of those wrenching laughs that threatens to turn into a sob. Years ago, Dean had made up a series of rules that the three of us had quoted to each other whenever we hung out. Rule number 8: When in doubt, deny.

"The thing is," Monica says softly, bolstered by what she feels is a shared memory between us, "I wanted to wear this great orange chiffon number and now, well..."

"Are you kidding?" I say. Any good will we shared with rule number 8 has flown, like a discarded wedge from a plastic coffee lid, out the window onto Storrow Drive.

"Did you think I'd wear a jacket and tie?" Monica snaps. She flips the ends of her platinum wig back.

"Michael—"

"Don't flatter yourself." Her voice drops two octaves. "You don't have *that* right to call me that and you never will."

Whenever Monica's real voice surfaces, I feel as if I'm talking to Linda Blair in *The Exorcist* and she's about to wrench her head around. I wait a moment, gathering my thoughts, girding myself. "Look, this is going to be hard enough as it is," I say in my most placating voice.

"Hard! Who's my wearing an orange chiffon dress going to be hard for? Dean loved that dress. Dean *bought* me that dress. Dean—" Monica has gotten herself so worked up, she starts to dry cough. "I'm wearing the orange chiffon and to hell with you and his parents," she says, coughing, her red manicured nails fanning around her mouth, like a bad imitation of a geisha. She coughs harder, bending slightly at the waist over the steering wheel, straining the seat belt. Monica knows how to play out a scene, I have to give her that.

"Are you okay?" I ask, but it's clear in the way I say it I don't care. But, Monica doesn't stop coughing. She looks at me, her eyes are watering. I start to get scared then.

"What is it? Are you choking?" I say, my voice getting louder.

Her coughing throws off her driving. The car swerves. Someone honks at us. It sounds like she's coughing up a lung.

"Oh my God, what can I do? Please, Monica. Tell me."

At that, the coughing abruptly stops. Monica glances over at me, smiling. "Oh kitten, I didn't know you cared," she says.

"You...you..." I sputter out. Several scathing retorts in my mind collide against each other into idiotic silence.

Monica says, "Tsk, tsk, you can do better than that, can't you?" Something about the way she raises her chin in profile, that fuck you, honey way she has about everything she says and does, makes me ditch my normal censoring mode.

"It must be hard never being who you want to be," I tell her.

"Trust me, sweetheart. Everything under the hood is the real deal and exactly what Dean wanted," she says, smiling broadly. She presses on the gas pedal of Dean's Mercedes, the gas pedal where Dean's foot in his polished loafer used to rest comfortably.

The car crosses over Marlborough Street. I'm so mad I'm wondering whether Monica would survive being pushed out of the car at this speed.

"Well, I'm glad *that's* over with," Monica says as we take a right on Commonwealth. She glances over at me. "You know what I'm talking about, right? Stage one?"

I stare at her.

"The anger stage? Kubler-Ross? Sister of Diana? Ain't no mountain high enough? Reach out and touch somebody's hand?"

"I can't believe Dean was ever with you," I say, turning to the window.

"Number 6, girlfriend," she says, but there isn't anything bonding in the way she says it.

Number 6: Sit back and enjoy the ride.

"What hotel are you staying at again?" Monica asks, checking out my expression. I'm supposed to stay with her at Dean's apartment on Comm. Ave. Monica tries to hold a straight face, but then laughs. "Just kidding, honey. It'll be like Cinderella and her wicked step-sister staying in the prince's house. Won't that be fun?"

It isn't. Well, maybe that's not the whole truth.

By the time we arrive, it's almost midnight, so I head straight for bed. I'm wide awake, though. How can I be in Dean's apartment without Dean? I touch the mattress as if it's the bed Dean had slept in, but it isn't. Monica's in that one. I'm in the guest room and tonight, I'm not even a guest of Dean's. I'm only here because Monica offered. Before I got here, I'd thought she would gloat over the fact that the apartment is now hers. But, she hasn't. She also threw me with all that Kubler-Ross stuff. Who thought that she'd be able to acknowledge that someone besides her could be grieving? Especially if that someone is me.

I miss Dean then. Normally I would've been whispering to him in the kitchen right now, asking him why Monica wanted me to stay. I start to cry, fueled on by the sheer frustration of being left without Dean and with Monica, but a few moments later I can hear an echo of my crying as if someone is mimicking me, making fun of me. My own crying catches in my throat as I try to listen to the other sounds coming from outside my room. I turn the light back on. The other crying goes on for a long time. Sometimes it gets softer, as if it's about to stop altogether, but then it starts up again like a lawn mower that won't quit after you turn it off. Finally, it tires itself out into silence.

That's when things get weird.

There's a soft tap on the door and it opens and suddenly Monica is in bed with me. She's still sniffling from her crying bout as she wraps her arms around me and pulls me in closer. I'm so stunned I can't move or say anything. Any impulse to push her away and tell her to get out is immediately squashed as I begin to feel gym-sculpted muscles pressing against me through her floral silk kimono.

"You're so beautiful," she murmurs in my ear.

"Monica," I say in my best stopping voice, in spite of the rising warmth my body is starting to feel and like.

"Don't say it," Monica says. "You loved him, I loved him. Love is love," she sighs, as she moves partly on top of me. I'm startled by how smooth her electrolysized cheek feels. Her mouth finds mine and for a second I'm confused by how urgent her tongue is; I'm not sure if it's driven by want or need. Monica feels my stiffness and backs off. She slowly moves off me and sitting up, tucks her legs demurely underneath her. She takes off her wig. Her wooly dark hair is close-cropped. I've never seen Monica without a wig. She goes from attractive to handsome in a second. Then she unties her kimono. She lifts my hand and placing it on her muscled chest, closes her eyes. Her hand, still on top of mine, guides my fingers across and down the hills and hard ridges. Maybe Dean was right about death. Maybe it simply makes us crave the warmth of the living, the concreteness of human touch. Or maybe I'd just gone too long without that.

I put my arms around Monica's neck and pull her down toward me.

*   *   *   *

Dean's parents don't show at the memorial. Either Monica called them back and laid it all out, or maybe she told them the memorial was postponed for some reason. I'm just glad there's not going to be a scene, other than the one Monica creates in the front row next to me, where the orange chiffon stands out against the wave of black suits like a buoy on a stormy ocean.

When I woke up, she was already in the shower. I avoided her in the apartment by staying in my room, pretending that my dressing was taking double the time it should've taken. Now that she'd talked to me about Kubler-Ross I wondered if she would want to process everything. I decided the best route was to low key it, pretend that I'd had many one night stands in my life and this probably wouldn't be the last. On the walk over to the church, though, she was surprisingly quiet, her face as blank as the grey sky above us.

At the reception after the memorial there are groups of men and women from the law firm Dean worked at. None of their black clothes shine from cheap polyester, like my black dress. Monica threads her way through the crowd toward me, drinks in hand. I hate to admit it, but she looks stunning. Handing me a martini, she takes a dainty sip of her own. "You know, he should be here," she says wistfully. "He was the conductor," she adds and even though she glances away, it isn't quick enough. I've seen that her eyes are wet.

"Your mascara's going to run," I say quickly.

"Revlon," Monica says and tells me that it's the kind that doesn't smear from crying. She dabs a little with a balled up tissue. "Listen, about last night," she says.

"Do you know these people?" I ask her. "I don't know these people."

"Carolyn, I'm talking," Monica says. "Look at me."

This makes me want to stick my head in a nearby bowl that has shrimp the size of my hand. Somehow I manage, though, to look straight at her, at her broad nose and exquisite cheekbones.

"What?" I ask her, as if I don't know.

"Carolyn," she says.

"Okay, okay," I tell her and then my practiced script rolls out. "Don't worry about it. I mean it was great, but it wasn't anything." I try to keep my voice level, lighthearted. "Let's just chalk it up to the stress of the memorial or something."

"You're okay, then?"

"Definitely," I say. But I'm not. It's as if something was taken from me before I was ready to give it up. It's the same feeling I got when Dean gave me a sweater for a birthday gift and it was the wrong size. I didn't even like the damn sweater–it was boxy. "I'll take it back," Dean said, throwing it into the box again.

"You know what this is, don't you?" Monica says and pauses. Her eyes, still a bit wet, sparkle. "This is one of life's little mysteries." I immediately drain what's left in my glass. Monica eyes me the whole time. "That's what Dean would say and you know it," she says. Rule number 1, stated whenever something inexplicable and joyful happened at the same time: This must be one of life's little mysteries.

"That pharmacy shit of yours isn't going to hold up," Monica says and dabs frantically under my eyes. "Look up. Look up," she urges me, her face so close I can smell olives and gin. Her eyes are wet too, but she's more intent on fixing me up: wetting the same used tissue with the tip of her tongue and lightly brushing under my eyes. That quick sighting of her tongue brings a rush of last night's gender bender back to me and I feel my face (and body) flushing with warmth all over again.

"Stop it," I tell Monica and push away her hand. I try to take a sip of my martini but the glass is empty.

"Next stop South Station," Monica says abruptly and grabbing my glass makes her way through the crowd to the bar. I can see several people's faces as Monica glides through them, her head held up high, her hips swaying, doing her runway walk. A couple of the more conservatively dressed men shake their heads and smirk. If Monica sees them, she doesn't show anything. In that moment, she becomes a marvel to me as she stands up taller and swings her hips even more. I realize then that I've had the briefest glimpse of what Dean was attracted to in her: the ability to rise above.

Monica comes back, cocktails in hand. Two of the Ken dolls give us rude stares. For that one second I wish I was more like Monica. I wish I could yell at all these people to go to hell, you didn't know Dean, go home, go away. I know if I ask her to, Monica would say those things and more in her loudest, most irritating voice.

Monica jerks her head in the general direction of the room. "What do you say we get wild, hmm?" She raises her eyebrows up and down. "Knock it back sweetheart," she says. I do, and for the first time all afternoon the martini feels ice-warm and comforting as it slips down my throat. She reaches out to take my glass, but I grab hers instead.

"My turn," I say.

I turn my back on her and start to walk toward the bar and that's when I hear from behind me a loud, "Toot toot." I know what she's doing, but I turn around to see anyway. She's standing there, one hand perched on her small hip, her other arm crooked in the air, her hand making a pulling motion, just like Dean did every time we drank martinis and were about to, what Dean called, "get on the teeny train." "Once you get on, you never get off," he'd say, the conductor of us all. Monica yells out again, "Toot toot." Conversation has completely died around us as if someone has fainted. I watch as Monica's hand hangs suspended in the air. It's one of those moments that can make or break the possibility for two lives to go on. I push my way back through the other mourners and when I reach Monica, she wraps her arms around me and pulls me in close.

"Oh God," she whispers into my crushed ear. "What will we do?"

Your Mother's Questions

Reginald Dwayne Betts

Have you ever had sex with a man?
Were you raped? Abused in any way?
You want the details, the camera to pan.
Have you ever had sex with a man?
You want the lens to focus on a span
of space where you imagine I didn't abstain.
Have you ever had sex with a man?
Were you raped? Abused in any way?

The rate of HIV is so much higher in prison.
I mean how did you deal with homosexuals?
We talked, but I've only had sex with women.
The rate of HIV is so much higher in prison.
Your daughter's voice on the phone, the rhythm
of her moans made masturbation natural.
The rate of HIV is much higher in prison
I mean how did you deal with homosexuals?

A lot of men come home and don't tell.
Even if you did, you wouldn't tell me.
Should I craft an elaborate tale?
A lot of men come home and don't tell.
The four of them rushed one cat's cell,
bent his body into a question mark. See?
A lot of men come home and don't tell.
Even if you did, you wouldn't tell me.

A Little Magic and a Lot of Faith

Patricia Eldridge

I could tell the time was coming, the time when I would tell my son my HIV status. Many times over the years, I struggled with whether or not I should tell him I was HIV positive, or what to say. Because I never had peace about the decision, I simply tabled it for another time. In the meantime, however, I did begin to build my foundation. I had always told my son to be careful with people's blood, especially Mommy's. I told him blood was dirty and it could carry germs that could make him sick.

I also talked to him about Magic Johnson. My son loves basketball and he knows all the great players, past and present. Magic has always been one of his favorites. Magic has also always been one of mine, ever since the time of short shorts, long socks, and big afros. I loved Magic. He was my hero. Now he is my hero in another arena as well. I used him as my building block in talking to my son about HIV.

The innocence of a child is so amazing. They don't come with preconceived notions about diseases. They don't have irrational fears and attitudes. They aren't judgmental. When I talked to my son about Magic, he was concerned and sounded sorry to hear that some people had treated him badly because he was HIV positive. I told him how AIDS kills a lot of people, but luckily, we have some medicines that help some people like Magic to stay healthier. Periodically I would find ways to revisit this conversation. I wanted to be sure he knew the facts about HIV. How you get it and how you don't. In addition, we talked about the stigma and the way some people felt about it.

I say I knew the time was approaching because I felt it in my spirit. Over a period of two weeks several people, all of whom did not know each other, asked me out of the blue when I was going to tell my son. I began to think about that question seriously and considered how and what to tell him.

It wasn't 100 percent clear to me until a situation arose that made me realize by not telling my story it was costing people their lives. By not sharing my experience and knowledge I was denying others real lifesaving information they needed. Granted, we all have some basic facts about HIV/AIDS. However until you put a face to it, a familiar face, a healthy face, it is surreal.

During this time, I went with a friend of mine to get tested. She found out the man she was dating was HIV positive. He had not told her, much like the person who had infected me. I told her my story and encouraged her to get tested. By the Grace of God, she was fine. I was able to see, in an intimate way, how important it was for me to share my experience with others. I knew in order to speak out I had to tell my son first. I didn't want to have someone else to tell my son my status before I did.

> *2 Timothy 1:6-7: Hence I remind you to rekindle the gift of God that is within you through the laying on of my hands; For God did not give us the spirit of fear but a spirit of power and love and sound mind.*

I went to the Youth Pastor at my church for counseling. I was an emotional wreck and didn't know how I could do this. God told me to weave a net of support, and that He would not let my son fall. I began by calling everyone that knew my status to tell them I was preparing to tell my son. I asked them if I could count on them to support him. I wanted to see if they could offer him a safe place to come and talk about his feelings and ask questions if needed. Of course, they all said yes.

When I went to speak to the Youth Pastor, I didn't know what to expect. As we talked, I gained a new sense of peace. I came to realize that in telling my son now, he would be able to see my walk of faith. I realized that is what was important to me. I wanted him to understand the faith that has brought me, us, this far. I don't know if I will ever develop AIDS or if AIDS will kill me. But I do know that God has done many miracles in my life and He continues to do so. My Youth Pastor offered to be there when I told my son. I thanked him and considered his offer. I decided that in my situation I wanted to tell my son in a very casual atmosphere.

My son and I talk quite a bit on a regular basis to each other and have a strong relationship. I wanted him to feel comfortable in the space we were in for him to be able to react. I knew he might have lots of questions and would be worried about me dying. He asked me about death when he was younger. I told him no one knows when they are going to die, and we live here on earth until Gods feels that our job is finished. I was prepared to revisit this conversation.

I sat down on the carpet for a game of cards. After a few rounds, I began the conversation by talking about Magic. After my stuttering a few times, my wise 8-year-old son asked me.

"Mom, what are you trying to say?"

I took a deep breath. "You remember what I told you about Magic Johnson and HIV?"

"Yes." He answered.

"And about how HIV can cause AIDS and many people can die from that?"

"Yes."

"But there are medications people take in order to help keep them healthy like Magic Johnson. Do you remember how I told you some people treated Magic when they found out he had HIV because they were afraid of HIV?"

"Yes."

"I just wanted to tell you that I also have HIV, like Magic."

He sat there thinking about what I had just said before finally asking if he had HIV as well. I told him that he didn't. I explained to him how I had to take medicine while I was pregnant and how God had protected him. "That is why I am always telling you what a miracle you are."

"Oh" he answered and trailed back into thought. After a moment of silence he sat down in my lap, put his arms around my neck in order to give me a big hug and said, "I don't care if you have HIV, because I love you!"

Without these three ingredients: power, love, and a sound mind, I would have never been able to tell my son I was HIV positive. I had been preparing him for a long time, and I had been preparing myself. I have learned to weather the elements, but I wanted to protect him. I wanted him to know the miracles that God has performed in both of our lives. I wanted him to see the goodness of God and that He is real. God spared my son's life when he was born and he saved it when he was baptized. I have seen God's spirit in my son in the bravery he has shown. When I told him I had HIV, he climbed up in my lap, hugged me and told me he didn't care if I had HIV. That was love. When I had a conversation with him later and told him I felt I had been called to speak about HIV, I put forth some hard questions to him. I asked if it would hurt his feelings if people didn't want to play with him, or if they told him I was going to die soon? He answered quite honestly and said yes. That is sound mind.

In my fear and natural instinct to want to protect my son, I asked if it was still okay if I went and did speaking engagements on HIV where I would reveal my status. His response? "Yes because they need to know! They need to know not to be scared!" That is power.

A few months later, I took him to a church to see Magic Johnson speak. I asked Magic to tell us how he told his children he was positive and ended up recounting my story. My son got to hug his hero and mine that day. It is a moment I will never forget, neither will he. As a matter of fact, he said he was going to write his autobiography starting at that moment.

SECTION II

So Young Pretty

Believe Them When They Say

Arisa White

You are pretty; they come with pretty things to match you. believe
them like you are the fourteen year old who got a back alley abortion
with chunks of fetus still left in your uterus, a grave of spoiled flesh

Was I black and ugly?

pretty are you to the Jewish guy who fucks you in a warehouse,
doggy-styled, dry, face against the grate for balance;
you cry when you see his footprints up and down your pants

Was I crazy in love?

the drug you are the pretty of the schizophrenic lover who snorts
coke off your pubic bone, while his friends watch him insert
vacuum attachments into your frightened pussy

Why did he do that to me?

pretty girl you are whose uncle comes from the Dominican Republic
and molests you at the dinner table; you're even the mother loving
you years later who says, we all must go through it

Why is this what they leave for me?

so young pretty you are so tight you are virgin mythologized
left broken to cup the spilling of a positive penis, from your
edges comes no cure, you meet your adolescence with AIDS

Who would touch me like this?

pretty clitoris clipped and sewn, military shotgun shattered,
vaginal walls, your community cannot stand the smell
of your shards; you are the bruised pretty, punched and beaten
to miscarry an undesired girl

Why am I here?

you are the vagina who never stops bleeding whose ovaries
scream and drop eggs as it pleases, your uterus diagnosed
hysterical; you are without the possibility of children

Am I?

you are pretty Karen, dirty diseased cunt, twat, pussy, so fat,
so wet, so pretty with your ocean stench, raped and ravaged hole,
unhealing wound, witch you harlot, mother, jezebel, hussy, puta,
virgin, lezzie, dyke, believe them you are pretty, pretty, pretty.

A Question of Survival

Evie Shockley

*it was the drugs that were making the children ill and the children
had been enrolled on the secret trials without their relatives' or
guardians' knowledge...to be free in new york city, you need
money.*

> —jamie doran, "new york's hiv experiment,"
> http://news.bbc.co.uk/2/hi/programmes/this_world/4038375.stm

are we defined   by what we   can survive or   what we can't?   some of us
    can test toxins   on colored orphans: can ask them   to swallow what
their bodies will   reflexively push up   or down and   out until their
    muscles clench around   the memory of   water and their   limbs thin and
tremble like twigs   in winter. some   of us can't.   some of us   can learn to
    gulp down drugs   before we're old   enough to spell   f.d.a.—while still
too small and   silent to be   considered consenting: can   drink exotic cocktails
    and live to   teach the doctors   a thing or   two about dosage.   and some of
us can't. what   would darwin say?   ask miss evers.   ask her boys.

Tiger Claw

Melanie Rivera

I didn't want to do it
that man took a fist to my sister
I had no other recourse
but that's not what charms is
chanting   dark rooms   chickens   gasoline
they're about protection, honey

women like us, that hurt like we do
keep jewelry boxes locked inside our skins
places in us that hold our gold
keep it safe from men like your daddy
that don't know how to handle it

now that's charms
locks to keep the evil out
sirens to warn
when danger is coming   teeth
sharp enough to drop the devil
where he stands.

Code of Honor

James E. Cherry

Teresa Randolph examined herself in the full-length mirror, flicked linen from her pants, tugged at the lapel of her blouse, ran a comb through her neatly cropped hair. Her uniform was crisp and creased the way a cop's uniform is supposed to be. She loved to hear her fellow officers joke about not standing too close for fear of being stuck, she being sharp as a tack. That was one of the good things the military taught her, pride in appearance. She kept telling herself over and over that everything was going to be alright; no *is* going to be alright. Maybe the test results were a false positive? She could always take it again. All of this time he had been playing her for a fool or as the homeboys say, "chumping her out" and she couldn't tolerate that. This was the day of reckoning where all soiled garments would be aired.

Teresa slammed the comb down on the dresser and derailed deliberations roaring through the tunnel of her mind, leaving a mass of musings twisted into a heap of frustration and seething anger. And the more she tried to conceal it the more it spilled over the rim of self-control, premeditated like the flow of volcanic lava. She had grown weary of diversionary games of denial with rationalizations of this could never happen to her and the grief that produces helplessness behind drawn curtains, locked doors and the avoidance of friends, enough was enough. She had exhausted all personal leave time and there were no more tears to waste. She was a cop and proud to be so; it was time to get back to work.

If anything, the last two weeks had given Teresa the opportunity to determine what was important, to separate wine from dregs, like ascending a ladder, each rung thrusting her into the fragile air of rationale where things were lucid and free. From this vantage point she could survey the 29 years of her life, measure goals against accomplishments, failures and victories, family and the future. She thought of her family: mom, dad, kid brother—still in her childhood home of Cincinnati. They had had her future all mapped out: ship her off to college for a degree and a husband. The degree and the concomitant accolades (magna cum laud) came as no surprise. But Teresa joining the U.S. Marines almost sent the Randolphs into cardiac arrest. And if that wasn't enough, the decision to become a cop after her four year stint in the armed services just about finished them off with a massive stroke. From that point on, whenever she phoned home with "great news," they always moaned "oh God" right before the big announcement.

It was on guard duty in the service that the idea of being an officer of the law first appealed to her, either that or back to school. A recruiter from the Memphis Police Department had left strong impressions after his departure; three months later she was in the academy and then on the force. She loved what she did. Only a handful of people could do what she could do. And being in the community, she was respected because Officer Teresa Randolph respected the people in the community. Her district was bordered by McCovey to the east and Orleans on the west with Lyons Court Public Housing dead center of both, affectionately known as the LC.

Initially, being Black and female she was tested from the moment she began her job, both in the squad room and on the streets. At one point she was about to throw up both hands regarding both situations until she solved the street problem by smacking around idiots and assholes who made lewd comments toward her, threatened her physical person or simply looked at her the wrong way; she wished she could do the same to some of her fellow officers who made comments about affirmative action, quotas and sleeping with supervisors within earshot.

She knew that after four years it was just a matter of time before the powers that be would want to stick her behind a desk in the supervision of others. But the streets were like a drug: intense, immediate and if not careful, addictive. One of the basic tenets of life on the streets was "handle your business first, call the cops last." If two guys had a beef, they would settle it amongst themselves by whatever means at their disposal. Reputation is everything whether in back alleys or boardrooms. If it wasn't for some of the people like the elder Mrs. Carraway, kids like Yusef and Keisha and sincere shopkeepers in the neighborhood, Teresa would have become as hard and calloused as some of the rapes, murders and assaults that comprised her days. She came seconds from joining some of her fellow officers in robbing a drug dealer of a hundred grand, reneging instead. One of the officers was driving a new Infinity now. And of course there was Robert.

Teresa placed her department issued revolver, badge and cap on the seat beside her in the car. She started the '98 Mustang, lit a cigarette, blew the smoke into her reflection in the rearview mirror.

It was in a court of law where she'd first met an attorney for the DA's office. Teresa was a witness for the State in a murder case involving a well known gang leader. It was a routine interrogation, she being no stranger to courtrooms but that thin, brown-skinned counselor in the well tailored suit made concentration on the task at hand very difficult. That lawyer was Robert Yarbrough. After the day's proceedings, he made an effort of running her down outside the courtroom, introducing himself and extending an invitation for the continuance of small talk over coffee in a nearby cafe. "I don't drink coffee," She had said demurely. "But I've been accused of running my mouth too much."

"I like the way the words sound when you run your mouth," he replied, enjoying the game of raised eyebrows, timorous smiles and the suggestive licking of lips. Besides, there was something about a woman in a uniform.

Coffee breaks evolved into months of dinners, movies, classical concerts, ballgames. They were considered a couple whether they knew it or not and three months later made it official with the consummation of their relationship. Robert had baked a chicken casserole, steamed broccoli, chilled wine and afterwards passionate kisses on the couch had evolved into mutually undressing in the hallway before pouncing on one another in the bedroom.

"Rubbers?" He frowned, echoed her query as if he'd never heard the word. "I don't think I have any." And resumed sucking her right breast.

"Wait."

Teresa reluctantly pulled away, like leaving a half piece of pecan pie on your plate having to rush for work; Robert panting for more nipple. Halfway back down the hallway, he heard the tearing of paper and when she re-entered the bedroom she rolled a condom upon his erect manhood and straddled him as if she'd returned from a long day at the office to finish sweetness deprived.

Their affair blossomed, plunging her deeper into more moments of nectar and love. And it wasn't just the sex. He knew so much about everything that he stimulated her intellect as well as her amorous passions. It was beautiful the way he tilted his head at an angle explaining mutual funds or the current regime in North Korea. In addition to his square shoulders, dark complexion, brown eyes, granite chin, he had a disposition that was polished with gentleness that made it easy to confide, trust in. She guessed Mom and Dad might end up in-laws after all. Career, man, only kids were needed to complete the circle. And even that came close to being a reality. One early morning night, both caught in convulsions of lovemaking, the rubber broke and so did Robert's self-control. Teresa still remembered the astonished look on his face and the queasy feeling that settled in the bottom of her stomach. After several pregnancy tests, a timely menstrual cycle and vows to swallow the pill, she, they, were in the clear.

But about six months into the relationship, the guys in the squad room smiled, giggled whenever they asked about Robert's wellbeing, as if sniggering was his surname. And whenever she pressed them on the source of their mischievous snorts, they simply shook their heads and moved away. One day, two weeks ago, Lieutenant Holt, half of pity and respect, witnessing her vexation, pulled her aside, removed his rank, and talked to her like a friend rather than a superior.

"Listen Randolph, your boy is on the DL."

He waited until the expanse of his words filled the chasm of understanding that separated the two of them. Instead, his cryptic epigram only divided them further.

"What?"

He stared deeply into her eyes, as if trying to see through her, eliminating all possibility of miscommunication. "That's right. DL. Down low."

A blinding light of understanding exploded in her eye. "You're crazy as hell."

Lieutenant Holt nodded in succession. "I been accused of that and it might be some validity to it. But one thing's for sho', I ain't no liar and I'm tired of people making jokes behind your back and you not knowing what was going on."

"You mean to tell..." Teresa gathered a far away look in her eyes as she turned away from the lieutenant, perceiving things only she could see. "...me that—"

He placed her hand on her shoulder. "Rumors been circulating for a while. But Riggs and Rogers go in this gay bar, The Other Side, looking for a dude passing bad checks and your boy, Yarbrough is in the joint kissing and being kissed by the dude that's been passing bad checks. They busted the dude who had been writing bogus checks and let your boy go after he showed his ID; you can't arrest a guy for kissing another guy, especially if the other guy wants to be kissed."

Teresa's bewilderment was entangled in a cacophony of silence. She could hear the lieutenant's voice droning in the background, his cheap cologne assailing her nostrils like the smell of frying foods but it was a Sunday morning, the same Sunday morning she discovered the women's garments in his dresser. He, in state prosecutor fashion, had convinced the people of the jury—she being the only one—that they belonged to his sister from Charlotte, who left them behind on her last visit. Teresa believed him. She was a woman in love and believed in him.

"So now you know." He gave her an empathetic look and admonished, "pull yourself together now. You're a cop. You still got a job to do." He left her alone.

A used car commercial blared from her radio and through rapid eye movements, Teresa realized she had been staring at her reflection for too long, a habit she'd become accustomed to. She readied the rearview mirror for driving, adjusted the volume on the radio. It was all coming together like pieces of a jigsaw puzzle. The late unexplained hours, the women's lingerie and now the test results. It made no difference that he'd been with another man. Sleeping with another woman would not have lessened the pain. Robert sowed; she reaped HIV. But what hurt most of all was the fact that the man she loved was a coward. His charm and wit, lies and deception. If he wanted to be gay, that's fine; she'd had gay guy friends in college and had her doubts about a couple on the force now. All he had to do was be honest. But his whole life was a fraud, a cover up, a joke and she was the last to know.

Teresa came to a stoplight, looked over at a quintet of youth congregating on street corners. She knew them by face and mannerism; they knew her by name. She knew that deals were going down. They didn't like one another but somewhere in the middle, they had to respect one another. She had busted three of the five before, knew the colors they'd sworn allegiance to, knew they were living warped versions of the American dream, knew that they were strapped with probably more firepower than she and they knew, and that word on the street was fuck with Teresa Randolph, or TR, as she was affectionately known, and she would fuck you up.

When the light changed, Teresa took her foot off the brake, rolled down her window and let her car crawl through the intersection. Her eyes shot hot steel daggers at the teens, and they in return, cold blank glares into her automobile. If either side flinched, someone would be leaking blood through bullet holes. It was a test of who would flinch first, a game as timeless as good guys and bad guys, if you could tell them apart.

Roll call was at 8:45. Teresa mashed on the accelerator, rolled up her window and saw the mouths of the drug dealers twist into angry forms in her rearview mirror. She wondered if the guys in the squad room would be glad to see her, had even missed her. She would summon up lies about vacation in this spot or the other. The time off was good for her though, made her realize how much she liked being a cop. But she was back. She was definitely back.

Teresa veered right onto Colerain and pushed Ella Fitzgerald into her cassette player. *How High the Moon* soared as she sped towards the north part of town. Robert's car was still in the parking lot of the apartment complex. She had no one else to blame but herself. She should've seen the signs, was trained to see them but had let a silly emotion like love blind her to everything. Emotion had no place in the life of being a good cop. If she took everything home with her that she experienced on the job, there would have been sleepless nights and very little sanity. She had been played and played to perfection. Fury momentarily rendered her blind, paralyzed all but breathing. She gathered up revolver, cap and badge, donned them all after exiting the vehicle, taking extra time to adjust her cap, polish her badge in the driver's window.

Teresa walked thirty yards to the front stoop as if she were measuring each step for weight and length. It felt good putting one foot in front of the other, as if the act itself was more important than the destination in sight. She noticed for the first time that the song of birds filled the air, a breeze carried the scent of a rose and that it was Spring. She rang the bell to apartment 343 and after several footfalls on the other side of the door, there was the silence of peephole examinations broken by the sliding of chains before the door was flung open.

Robert, hand still on the knob, framed the doorway in a white long sleeved shirt, red tie, black suspenders. His smile was like sunlight spilling upon the polished department issued shoes of Teresa. He brought a white coffee mug to his lips, swallowed. "Hey baby. This is a pleasant surprise." He checked his watch. "I've got a few minutes. Come on in." He opened the door wide, allowed her entrance, shut it behind them.

Mrs. Gromeyer's presence in the neighborhood each morning was as accurate as a Swiss timepiece. At a quarter to nine, she was always seen walking Happy, her French poodle who wore a vest with the letter H on it, for her health and for the sake of K-nine bodily functions. Halfway through her peregrinations, she heard a loud report akin to the backfiring of an automobile and stopped in her tracks, straining for additional sounds; Happy whined with trepidation, tried to hide behind his owner's leg. There followed the faint sound of breaking glass, as if a dish had accidentally fallen to the floor. She remained motionless for a few remaining seconds, curiously, until Officer Teresa Randolph emerged from apartment 343, softly closed the door behind her and straightened her cap.

"Good morning, ma'am."

Mrs. Gromeyer's mien transformed from a fainthearted frown into a soothing smile, her body relaxing into a non-defensive stance and even Happy wagging his tail, danced at his owner's feet.

"Oh, good morning officer," she replied diffidently. Then to her four-legged varmint, "Come along Happy. It's a beautiful day and we have much to do," as Officer Randolph self-assuredly brushed past her. Lieutenant Holt would be expecting her at roll call in five minutes.

Some Days Other than Sunday

Nancy Jackson

I used to love going to church on Sundays with Grandma
But then it started and getting me to go to church felt like a death
sentence
I was so scared, too scared for Grandma and me

At first it was just go clean up the youth ministry space
Then it was come inside my office
Then it became sit on my lap, then it became him wet
all down there between his legs

Then he started kissing me like a girl
And when I would fight Grandma to keep from going
She would beat me with a switch and say to her friends
I don't know what's gotten into that boy anymore

Then the sisters in the Amen Corner started looking at me
Like I was a sinner or something

That time when he first took my pants down and sat me on top of
his penis and wet me up all over my bottom was when I thought
maybe I was going to die

I couldn't tell Grandma, cause he said he would go down to the school
and make them take her job away from the janitor's service
I knew I couldn't let that happen to her, after-all what would become of us?

I spent many months trying to figure a way out, then came the new
Boy, Alvin, all proper and clean,
Preacher took one look at him and
I could see across the pews that I was getting a replacement

Didn't take long, a few months more
Then I over heard the Preacher inviting Alvin's old Auntie to
become a member of the congregation, all the while looking the boy
up and down

I was happy to be removed from the service to the church and to
be painted a backslider
And I never told a soul about that Preacher
But he sure wasn't no man of God

By the time we found out that I was seventeen
and HIV positive it was too late
The Preacher had moved on to some other community
Later we got word he had died from AIDS.

Isolation

Fred Joiner

hands are meant to be held,
but Death can hide in a hand
shake or in the breath
of a stranger's exhale

Gravity

Duriel Harris

He said he had cancer. He did.
But it was what he did not have that killed him.
It's like that. *Gravity takes.*

The flesh of his body thinned.
Skin fell in flakes.

Nothing left to fight...
We stood on the platform's yellow line,
waiting, rocking our heels, watching
the dingy glint of tracks for signs.
I saw a rat darting in and out of side pockets
pulling twine to make something underground.
I'm unraveling, he said.
I wished I had hopped the turnstile:
as if stealing small things
could bring small things back.

Ugo's Fear

Tony Medina

The girls cannot walk
the streets alone

I make sure they
are always together

or that Jabu is with them—
girls are not safe on the streets

I don't know where they get
the notion, but some of these boys,

and men as well, think attacking
young girls will cure them of AIDS

It is bad enough that we must
suffer through so much uncertainty

than to have people create such
dangerous superstitious beliefs

I grew up through such hard times
with passbooks and *European Only* signs

trying to keep me in my place, now AIDS
seems to be taking Apartheid's place

It is unfair; my children had to grow up
with Apartheid,

now their children have to live
with AIDS

Test Results

Dante Micheaux

The results of my latest test were non-reactive—
as if to say: up against this virus is my blood, non-reactive.

Testing has evolved and become so attractive.
No more three-week, stuck-in-the-mud, non-reactive

waits, the kind that make rays of life refractive
and force those around you to bud non-reactive

intellects. Gone are the emotionally inactive
doctors; they've been replaced by a flood—non-reactive

counselors desensitized to doling out reactive
results. I remember the word *stud*, non-reactive

as I was to it in my adolescence. Active
boys, my friends and I were, deaf to the thud non-reactive

vials made in sterilized beakers—proactive
teenagers far from the chewing cud non-reactive.

The Down Low

Curtis L. Crisler

I.
Tonya married Barry for the modulation
in his voice. It sang deeply to her vulva. He
was her first male and she gave him her cherri
in the sweet moments called heat. They became
the "one" that Genesis reveals Adam and Eve
to be. Under moonlight, above the rise of many suns
they begot three children. Life became Cinderella
mixed with crap-filled pampers, the closeness of two
people in one room—amplified silence and dust mites.
And when he would not touch her to make her ah
she cried, before discovering her hands were strange
lovers—smiled on the down low when Barry
opened the door to leave with the boys.

II.
When he on down low
his blue so high she can't hear him
squeal. The pillow muffles his harsh pound,

like Armstrong's mute on those slow rag-tunes,
fingering the tendrils in the gut. Going out with
T. J. and Monte, Barry loses his soul, splits cracks
of matrimony—he knows where to place the ah
he lost with Tonya. His compassion lays there
in his lies to wife, in wrinkled sheets of Comfort
Inn with other husbands, finding out who-da-man.
Barry fishes for man-eaters off this coastal
divide, hidden in half smiles and routine.

III.
It blindsides her like shark attack
or blitzing outside linebacker—a waiting
many women go about not knowing—waiting-
area many women encounter before finding out
diagnosis that a *straight* man can bend and
a *straight* man's still *straight* when crooked—
a "low-down-dirty-dog" that got his woman one
of highest on food chain of disease. Tonya thinks
how Lorena Bobbitt would attack, diagnose it—
she'd say, "Pull till the root is exposed,
then swing him this sway, sister."

Saving African Women and Children One Movie at a Time: Truth Masquerades as Fiction

Terry M. Dugan

The film adaptation of John le Carre's novel, *The Constant Gardner*, pitches the movie to American audiences as a romantic thriller. Both the book and the movie revolve around a courtly British diplomat, whose beautiful young wife, an attorney, and her male colleague, an African physician, are killed for documenting the lethal, unreported side effects experienced by Kenyan women and children during clinical trials for a miraculous new TB drug, Dypraxa. The heartbroken husband uses his cloak and dagger training to track down pharma's paid assassins who raped and decapitated his wife and tortured and burned her colleague. Both the book and the movie introduce a mass audience to the plight of African women and children who participate in clinical trials enduring dangerous side effects for useless treatments while the pharmaceutical companies pursue profits.

It's not surprising that a movie featuring nudity, exotic scenery, brutality, and blood thirsty villains would be popular in the United States, regardless of the important but didactic plot about the consequences of exposing the nefarious practices of big pharma in Africa. What is surprising is that major reviews in *The New York Times* and *The New Yorker* barely mention the acting and directing. Instead, they devote more space to describing the film as a polemical rant whose message was worthy but annoying. One newspaper reviewer predicts opinion page challenges to the film's dire view of pharmaceutical companies.[1] Another reviewer thinks that anger over using Africa to test experimental drugs would be easier to provoke in Europe with its exploitative colonial past, ignoring America's neocolonial present, where Africa is used as a hunting ground for oil and a dumping ground for AIDS drugs.[2]

Only one review, published in *The Nation* magazine, seriously considers the message. The reviewer notes that while outsourcing of clinical drug trials are increasing, the benefits for sick Africans and others in the developing world are not materializing. She agrees that ethical lapses are unfortunate, but risks are part of experimental drug trials and are necessary for researchers to learn and, ultimately, to save lives.[3] The reviewer overlooks the fact that all medical and behavioral researchers must follow the Nuremberg Code, and all of us have signed statements adhering to its principles, which define patient protections during experiments. This is a binding international protocol. The reviewer is probably aware that the Nuremberg Code was developed to prevent a repeat of the horrific experiments Nazi doctors conducted on their prisoners during World War II, but apparently does not think it should apply to pharmaceutical companies. (It does.)

The reviewer is also critical of the movie because it does not give specific information about the clinical trial of the fictional drug, Dypraxa. This is partly a fault of the medium. Presenting detailed information without talking the audience into a stupor would require a very long animated PowerPoint slide show.

But the book does an admirable job of showing the effects of a botched clinical trial. In a pivotal scene very early in the novel, the crusading young attorney gives birth to a stillborn baby at a hospital used by residents of the shantytowns in Nairobi. She is visited by her husband's superior, who is shocked when he sees her nursing a black newborn baby. "He's not mine," she explains, "his mother can't feed him." His mother had taken part in the failed trial of Dypraxa and now lay dying in a bed across the room. The attorney lists the reasons why the woman is dying: overcrowding, undernourishment, filthy living conditions, and greedy men in white coats. She explains that for the first few days, they visited twice a day because they were terrified. They prodded her, read her numbers, and talked to the nurses. But now they were gone. The scene appears in the movie, too, but the visual distraction of seeing a beautiful bare breasted white woman nursing a tiny black baby on a huge screen undermines the dialog about the aftermath of the clinical trial.

Information that appears in the book but not on the screen is the extensive disclaimer that John le Carre included at the end of the novel. All fiction carries a boilerplate paragraph insisting that everything in the story is made up. *The Constant Gardener* has a three-page litany of disclaimers and explanations. For example, descriptions of the British diplomatic core are generically true but all positions and names are fictitious. More importantly, he states: "There is no Dypraxa, never was, never will be. I know of no wonder cure for TB that has recently been launched on the African market or any other—or is about to be—so with luck I shall not be spending the rest of my life in the law courts or worse."[4]

On a more ominous note, le Carre continues: "As my journey through the pharmaceutical jungle progressed, I came to realize that, by comparison with reality, my story was as tame as a holiday postcard." In the one and one-half pages devoted to naming the experts and consultants who assisted him when he was researching his novel, le Carre reveals the core of his story:

"...medical opinion continues to be insidiously and methodically corrupted by the pharmagiants..."[4]

John le Carre's novels are known for excursions into speculative realism when fictional characters are caught up in real events. There are numerous real examples of ethically challenged clinical trials in Africa. The reviewer from *The Nation* cites one from Thailand that took place many years after le Carre wrote the novel, which was published in 2000. The other reviewers didn't take the message seriously enough to investigate further. But there were clinical trials conducted in the 1990s in Africa that closely parallel the fictional Dypraxa trial, including the mysterious deaths of whistleblowers, cover ups of lethal and toxic side effects, ethical breaches in recruiting patients, and physicians paid to shill worthless remedies. Here are just two egregious examples.

Philanthropy or Pharmacolonialism?

In 1996, Pfizer sponsored a clinical trial of an oral antibiotic, Trovan, for children suffering from a deadly form of meningitis in a hospital in Kano, Nigeria. There was no evidence that informed consent was obtained from the parents of the children. But there was evidence that the approval letter from the hospital ethics committee was backdated because the hospital did not have an ethics committee when the clinical trial started.[5]

The Nigerian physician who was listed as the principal investigator claimed that he was only minimally involved in the conduct of the trials but admitted that he backdated the ethics approval letter. At the time, Nigeria was dealing with a meningitis epidemic and Doctors Without Borders were at the Kano hospital prescribing approved antibiotics. Were they angered that an unproven drug was given to children when licensed antibiotics were readily available? Did they note serious side effects that were ignored by the trial monitors? In his disclaimer, John le Carre specifically mentions that consultants with Doctors Without Borders gave him invaluable information about the conduct of clinical trials in Africa. It is entirely possible that the facts about this trial shaped some aspects of le Carre's fictional Dypraxa trial.

In 1997, Pfizer won approval for Trovan from the FDA, but only for adult use. The drug was projected to gross up to one billion dollars a year. Trovan had never been prescribed for American children with meningitis and was not approved for children. According to an account in *The Washington Post*, by 1999, reports of deadly side effects, including liver damage and death, forced the FDA to place stringent limitations on the use of Trovan. The drug was banned in Europe.[5]

If le Carre based some of his narrative on the Trovan case, he would have finished writing his novel well before the newspaper article, published in 2000 in *The Washington Post*, recounted the illegal experimentation on Nigerian children as part of a larger investigation into pharmaceutical companies testing drugs in developing countries. The response to this revelation was unprecedented. There were street demonstrations in Nigeria, a panel of Nigerian medical experts was convened to review Pfizer's conduct, and lawsuits were filed in the United States on behalf of the Nigerian children who participated in the trial.

In 2006, *The Washington Post* learned that the Nigerian panel of medical experts produced a lengthy report recommending sanctioning Pfizer for violating international law in 1996 and strengthening laws to prevent another illegal clinical trial. But the report remained confidential for five years. American lawyers believed there were only three copies of the report. One copy was stolen from a Nigerian government safe. A second copy was in the possession of a Nigerian official who died. In an instance where fiction shapes the interpretation of facts, an American lawyer described these circumstances as "a mystery novel...like John le Carre."[5]

In 1997 in Kampala, Uganda, a clinical trial assessing the effectiveness of AZT compared to Nevirapine in preventing the transmission of the HIV virus from infected mother to newborn began. AZT, the first antiretroviral drug used against AIDS, had already been proven to reduce transmission but required several precisely timed doses during pregnancy and many follow up visits. Nevirapine was a newer class of antiretroviral drug and was approved for treating AIDS in adults in the United States under the name Viramune. Nevirapine was supposed to block the transmission of HIV from mothers to babies with a single dose. In resource-constrained sub Saharan Africa, where 600,000 infants a year are born exposed to HIV, this is the closest thing to a magic bullet.[6] Based on preliminary results from this one study, researchers published an article claiming Nevirapine was safe to give to pregnant women and newborns and was just as effective as AZT. Two years later, independent international monitors found that the trial was flawed, and the rates of spontaneous abortion of pregnancies, liver damage, and drug resistance were misstated. Clinical trials of Nevirapine were suspended temporarily.[7] John le Carre had many contacts among humanitarian observers and international medical corps members. Some would have been on the ground in Kampala during such a critical clinical trial and may have told him in confidence about these problems long before they were uncovered by the independent monitors.

Two years after *The Constant Gardener* was published, a technical report reviewing the safety and effectiveness of Nevirapine prompted the World Health Organization (obliquely referred to as "clueless" in le Carre's disclaimer) recommended its use in Africa for pregnant women and newborn babies.[8] Four physicians, two of whom were paid consultants for Nevirapine's manufacturer,

Boehringer Ingelheim, wrote the report. The other two physicians had been involved in maternal transmission of HIV studies that raised serious concerns among their colleagues. In the United States, the National Institutes of Health (NIH) directed another investigation of the conduct of the Nevirapine clinical trials in Uganda. NIH researchers found serious scientific and ethical flaws, including the underreporting of thousands of severe reactions to the drug. The FDA approved Nevirapine as a "pregnancy category C" drug because animal studies demonstrated adverse effects on the fetus and there were no well-controlled studies in humans. But Nevirapine could be prescribed where the potential benefits outweighed the risks.[9]

On June 19, 2002, President George Bush announced a $500 million initiative to save African mothers and newborns with a single doses of Nevirapine. One month later, NIH released its report to the Ugandan government containing detailed information about the ethical and scientific violations in the Nevirapine trials. But in the United States, Dr. Edmund Tramont, chief of the NIH's AIDS Division, altered the conclusions of his staff's negative reports on Nevirapine. He defended his actions, claiming it was important to encourage Africans to fight AIDS, especially when the President was about to visit them. Apparently, the political benefit outweighed the risk to pregnant African women and newborns.[10]

By 2004, the reports of the adverse reactions and ethical misconduct prompted the Medicines Control Council, a group of South African health officials, to refuse to give Nevirapine to pregnant women. South Africa was already administering AZT to prevent maternal transmission of HIV.[11] Newspapers all over the world carried variations on the headline, "A common treatment given to pregnant women with HIV is dismissed as too risky." Dr. Joep Lange, the president of the International AIDS Society and the paid consultant for Boehringer who had authored the WHO report, vilified the South African officials who had voiced objections to Nevirapine.[8] Dr. Lange received extensive press coverage for his allegations without one reporter bothering to investigate his financial links to the drug manufacturer.

The release of the movie based on *The Constant Gardener* should have been an opportunity to discuss the growing problem of profit-driven clinical trials and drug research. Perhaps most critics assumed that ethical lapses and scientific manipulations could only happen in Africa. But a report, released by the Alliance for Human Research Protection in 2005, found that 48 AIDS drug experiments were conducted in America beginning in the 1990s on foster children in seven states.[12] Toxic drugs, including Nevirapine, and experimental vaccines were given to children as young as six months old without adequate consent or oversight by an independent advocate.[13]

Drugs like Trovan and Nevirapine lack a sexy love story, lush tropical settings, telegenic whistleblowers, and suitably slimy corporate villains. No beautiful dead bodies, no cliff hanging exposes, just business as usual in the world of big pharma. It seems that pharmaceutical weeds need constant gardening.

References

1. Scott, A.O. "Digging Up The Truth In a Heart of Darkness." *The New York Times*. August 31, 2005.

2. Lane, A. "Officers and Gentlemen: *The Constant Gardener*." *The New Yorker*. September 5, 2005.

3. Shah, Sonia. "*The Constant Gardener*: What the Movie Missed." *The Nation*. August 30, 2005.

4. LeCarre, J. 2001. *The Constant Gardener*. New York: Simon & Schuster.

5. Stephens, Joe. "Panel Faults Pfizer in '96 Clinical Trial in Nigeria." *The Washington Post*. May 6, 2006.

6. Antiretroviral Drugs for Treating Pregnant Women and Preventing HIV Infection in Infants. 2004. Geneva, Switzerland.

7. Timeline for HIVNET012 Clinical Trial, Audits and Investigation. 2005. www.hivnet.gov.

8. World Health Organization. Antiretroviral drugs and the prevention of mother-to-child transmission of HIV infection in resource-limited settings. Report of a Technical Consultation, February 5-6, 2004. Geneva, Switzerland.

9. Viramune (Nevirapine): A Complete Guide, www.aidsmeds.com.

10. Solomon, J. "AIDS Research Chief Rewrote Safety Report." Associated Press. December 15, 2004.

11. LaFraniere, S. "South Africa Rejects Use of AIDS Drug for Women." *The New York Times.* July 14, 2004.

12. "New Evidence Uncovered About AIDS Drug/Vaccine Experiments on Foster Care Infants and Children." 2005. Alliance for Human Research Protection. www.ahrp.org.

13. Solomon, J. "Researchers Tested AIDS Drugs on Children." Associated Press. May 5, 2004.

SECTION III

Pulsing
Somewhere Distant

those were my friends
dead people
like martin luther king jr
& harriet tubman
I saw them
they were around me
we talked
they would say baby you gonna get better
don't worry "

MOMMY KNOWS
MOMMY KNOWS
MOMMY KNOWS

SWEET BABY

HARRIET'S COME
TO HELP YOU AGAIN
HARRIET'S
HERE
DON'T WORRY BABY

YOU'VE SEEN
RIVERS LIKE THIS
BEFORE
YOU'VE KNOWN

PAIN LIKE THIS BEFORE

YOU STEPPED
INTO THE WATER YOU'VE
CROSSED YOU'VE
MADE IT
TO THE OTHER SIDE "

marlon marlon marlon   *noira*
this person is not dead to me
you achieve you

PASS IT ON

YOU SAID
SIMPLY
SILENTLY
WITH YOUR EYES
REMEMBER HARRIET?
"WADE IN THE WATER CHILD IF
YOU WANT TO GET
TO THE OTHER SIDE" "

death
can be transcended by memory

these people are not dead to me

when I look at their images I
don't see death I see
extremely

EMPOWERING
LIFE-GIVING force
&
I know that

I can achieve that too
&
PASS THAT ON "

MARLON TROY RIGGS
FEBRUARY 17 1957/
APRIL 5 1994

i shall not be removed - the life of marlon riggs -
karen everett california newsreels 1996 "

Scope

Alan King

it's selfish to be earth-
bound when you should be
pulsing somewhere distant
or constantly reminded
that a Hitman lurks among
your T cells

or the fact you're positive
keeps you on the other end
of a sniper's lens

Excerpt from EFFLUVIUM*

Arisa White

Prose Piece I

The first thing Neisey says to me, when I get off the plane from Ghana, you have to go see Karen. I say, I will. I say, I will. I went off to the Berkshires, in the mountains, to administer to dancers and didn't go. To what would have been the final time I would have seen you. You died four weeks later. I didn't go. I didn't even take a bus down to your funeral. I could have borrowed the money. I didn't ask. Anyone would have given me bus fare.

Prose Piece II

I cannot even recall how you look without assistance from a photo. Every image pulled is you frozen by a camera's lens, smiling. Last year, Neisey gave me a book, glued photos of me when I was a baby and there is one with you. You holding me; I dressed in a sailor suit. This is how I remember you now. The last time you came around, you were wearing a wig. Your skin that of a doll, tight and shiny, a manufactured brown you find on fake things, on no living skin. I don't know if I hugged you. I feel my eyes held you from a distance, blinking out the questions of where you been, why you look like that, are you ok, how are you? Then, I did not know what made you sick. You grinned at all the faces that smiled. You were in white. And I know I said hello, I know I must have said hello.

Prose Piece III

I still have not visited your grave. I am afraid to see people wilt before tombstones, whole bodies weeping, remembering what these dead ones left behind. And the silence of the cemetery swallows this all, people appear as pantomimes of mourning. I do not want to talk to you in the open. The wind is a thief. The dirt takes everything and buries it. And then we would have to clear the dirt from our mouths. For three years, you've been buried; I've been savoring this sorry as if it were the red in Hojo's mouth. Maybe this is how I would have begun, wiping my lips, at your bedside, the way you did after you kissed Hojo, in the elevator of your mom's apartment building, it smelled of urine and beer and there you and Hojo stood, eyes meeting eyes, I looking up at your profiles, you sucking on a red piece of hard candy, he asked if he could have some and you brought your mouth to his, your tongue rolled the candy behind his teeth, he sucked on your sweet, and I thought that was the perfect way to share.

*A series of prose poems

Visiting Hours Are Over

Truth Thomas

There are no gay, straight, down low, get high, protected, unprotected sex questions for you now. Now, a morphine drip drains its indifferent bladder in your arm. Now a monitor's beeps get sleepy in the shadow of your cough. So many came to see you today—so many came and left, though you will not remember: the priest (the only one who touched you); the nurse (who slurped your soup and juice). I wonder if they knew you only had one boyfriend (Solomon in high school, who told you that he loved you. Solomon in high school, who messed with college girls). Well it doesn't matter now. You are only brown sheets here, bowing to a jealous full-blown God. The only points to make are hypodermic. Visiting hours are over, but I am here. I am nothing if not faithful.

Tari

Dike Okoro

We did not see his corpse
Nor did we read the coroner's report
After the rain brought us
To his mother's house
Four old men sat outside
Talking, washing pain with gin
Six old women dressed in black
Sat on the couch in the living room,
Not a word heard
Men in the backyard skinned a goat,
Like poems edited for brevity and clarity
Young women washed the rice in large metal pots
And cut the tomatoes to prepare the stew
This was the house where Tari
Grew up chasing paper kites in the sky
And kicking orange as soccer
In the front yard
This was the house where Tari returned
From high school graduation at 20

And opened a food store
Ending any dream of seeing the walls of a university
The same food store where
The girls who stayed out late in the streets after dark
Frequented with their rich and promiscuous company
The men who repaid Tari for his generosity
In handing them beer on credit with
Girls for the night
And what did the young men know then
When the sermon of the day was that the berry was sweeter
Without the skin
Now the story of the young man
Will not be told by the coffin lying
Before the silent mother and his gagged wife
Today nobody will think of the enemy
Who slipped in after sperm exchange and
Other ways no one alive can tell with certainty
His brother K says it was pneumonia when I asked
An honest confirmation baked to keep me from knowing
But it was the oldest man in the family
The one who still remembers when Tari and me
Ran the yard down from dawn till dusk
Chasing the roosters for fun and aiming sticks
At ripe mangoes hanging in trees who
Called and sat me down on the concrete
To tell me it was the killer running its course like a hag
Having defied all applications by local herbalists and hospitals
That took the young man we all called Pele for
His antics on the football field now a biting memory

Grenades

Myronn Hardy

Ecru material bought at the market.
She sews a dress   spins.
Her husband is a shower

of bullets unseen for a year.
He lives in the capital.
Everything destroyed   rumor.

Brazil is Andromeda poured
in porcelain. She drinks
    the body charged

minerals   incandescent.
She has to leave Angola.
Her husband won't return

to their village   nothing.
Their son wanders treeless
groves   *Onde é meu pai?*

The Atlantic makes her sick
yet she still spins. The coast
cuts her eyes. The ship

docks   she spins faster.
The New World turns her
away for the grenades

in her blood. Thrown
there by a man who wears
whores like skin. She thinks

of her husband while watching
water froth against the
ship   returning. Home

a continent as hospice.
It had been so for her three
sisters. Their bodies gradually

gaunt   hollow until dust.
This plague lures locusts to feast.
Ashes   blow it all up.

Laughter Lost in the Hills

Ifeanyi Ajaegbo

He clamped his teeth together when I touched him. His skin was hot, like the back of the tin kettle sitting on a small iron tripod in the corner of the room. His forehead was coated with little drops of sweat, slender rivulets running down the sides of his face and disappearing into the pillow under his head.

"*Dim*," I called him softly.

His eyes flicked open and looked at me. They blazed as if all the fires of hell burned behind them. His jaws twitched as if he wanted to say something to me but could not.

"Please," I begged him, not sure what I was pleading for. Faced with circumstances beyond us, we seldom knew what to do.

He nodded. The vacant look in his eyes left no doubt in my mind that even he did not know what I begged for.

"*Obim*," he said. His voice hoarse and soft, almost stolen by the illness that was killing him slowly.

I reached out and took his hand in both of mine. Unlike the rest of him, it was cold.

"They say I cannot die... in peace too? In my own house?" He asked, the anger forming a haunting backdrop to his pain.

"Yes, *dim*."

I never wanted to tell him. The rejection by his own people would be worse than the death he knew waited for him. But there was no way I could explain having to move him to the deserted hut at the outskirt of the village.

"Yes," I said, blinking back the tears that stung my eyes.

"I cannot live out this ... this life? In peace?"

"They are afraid *dim*?"

"Of me? Now?"

"No, not of you. They are afraid of what is killing you."

"But it cannot touch them." He cried out, his voice made stronger by his anger.

"They do not know that *dim*," I told him. "They do not know that it kills from the inside. Not the outside. And they are afraid."

He was silent. His breath coming in short rasps.

They were afraid. The fear etched into their foreheads reflected in their eyes the night they came to tell me he could die among his people. The knock on the door was furtive, as if the person outside was afraid of waking whatever demon slumbered inside the house. I rose from fireside, where I was stoking the flames to boil water. Outside, I saw the representatives of the woman of the village, led by Egoke, the village matriarch. I greeted her kneeling down. She responded, her voice firm despite her great age. I wondered why they came. I was not surprised when Egoke told me that Ukela must not die in the village. Listening to her explain the fear Ukela's illness had brought on the village, I wanted to hate her. I realized then that pain and anxiety had stolen the strength to hate from me. I wanted to ask why did the women come to tell me that my husband could not die among his people. I wanted to ask how they could have forgotten so easily the man who did so much for the village. Instead I thanked her. I had resigned myself to all that life would throw at me. Bitter and ashamed, I turned away from them and closed the door in their faces, on their accusing eyes.

"Yes, *dim* they are afraid," I told him, walking around the bed to the other side.

"But this is my home," he protested.

"Yes," I agreed, not wanting to tell him that his illness had robbed him of the luxury of love from his people.

"It will be only for a short while."

I moved my hands under his armpits and almost pulled them away. His skin was hot, but I closed my mind to the heat and dug my hands deeper and helped him struggle to his feet. He felt so light; his brittle skin draped over his bones like a thin covering. He tried to grasp my shoulders with a shivering hand, but it slid off, falling limply to his side. His hairless head, once big with a shaggy mane of hair, tilted to one side. The taut skin of his skull gleamed against my shoulder.

He moaned at the effort of standing up. The sound of pain rolled around in the darkness of the room, an aftermath of evil that would not go away. His head moved slightly, as if he were listening to the sound of his pain flung back at him by every piece of furniture, every object in the room. Steadying myself to take what was left of his weight, I led him toward the door. Like two people entwined in a dance of the living dead, we moved around pieces of furniture.

The doorknob felt cold and unforgiving, but yielded to the twist of my wrist. The hinges creaked loudly in the darkness, the sound of a dying monster, swallowing the last drawn out echo of his moan. The breeze, long held at bay by the closed door, dashed into the house in a cold celebration of freedom. Everything in the night was cold. Everything, except his body, which was hot enough to scald.

Outside, the darkness was total and absolute, opening up to swallow us in a formless embrace. Behind us, the thunder of the door closing exploded into night. The sound was sudden, momentarily robbing me of breath. I stopped my next step mid-air and turned to look at the door. My eyes searched for the monster lurking in the dark. The door could not have closed itself. Nothing was there, except the population of shadows that peopled the darkness. I turned once more in the direction of the hut and we moved forward, trying to avoid pieces of rock jutting up from the ground in an obscene attempt by the earth to reach for the sky.

I looked at him.

Ukela's eyes were closed.

I wondered what he thought. If he thought anything at all. Perhaps just questions, each one an attempt to deny an obvious fate. We had talked about this whenever he had the strength to speak. He could not be dying. The thought of that eventuality stopped the breath as much as death. Denial. Not Ukela, the perfect husband and son. At least till his mother died. This man who never forgot his friends' birthdays and anniversaries. He visited his mother regularly beyond the hills just to be with her. My husband of the low voice, and even lower temper. Denial. I wanted to know why bad things happened to good people. I wanted to know why there was so much pain, so much agony in existence that was supposed to be so beautiful. Deny what was, perhaps it would cease to be.

I pulled my eyes away from his face and looked around me. A soft breeze ruled the night. It raced through the crowns of trees, caressing soft sighs from the leaves and the branches. The weeds and the grass grazed our ankles and knees as we passed, lush from a sprinkling of rain earlier in the evening. Droplets of water fell from overhanging leaves that brushed against our bodies as we staggered past. Occasionally, bats, owls and other night birds passed overhead, or swooped low off to one side, shrieking as if they felt and understood the pain deep inside; the agony. I looked at each swooping bird, each passing, hearing in each shriek shredding the night, a sealing of the bond of pain uniting man and nature; us and the darkness.

Every thing around us reminded me of home, a home we had already left behind. A home to which none of us would come back alive, and that was if we came back to it at all. Among my husband's people, a widow had no song. She was considered dead also, as soon as her husband died. She was not his heir; had no right to anything he owned. She just ceased to be. I wondered where home was now. And what would happen to me.

A moan pulled me away from my thoughts. Ukela had stumbled and was falling. He was there, entwined in my arms and held close to my body; the next breath he was gone. I dove for him, my fingers drawn into claws, missing his flailing arms. My heart sank at the harsh expulsion of breath as his body struck the ground. I fell to my knees on the ground beside him. Ukela lay on his back, staring helplessly at the night sky. He looked so helpless, lines of pain etched into his forehead. His eyes stared vacantly, past me at the night sky. He looked dead.

"I am sorry my husband," I said, choking back the sobs bubbling up from the well of despair inside.

There was no sign he heard.

I worked my fingers under his body, but could not lift him up. The journey from the house, the village had drained me of all strength. Frustrated, kneeling beside him in the cold night, I felt something stir inside. A deep-seated anger; a burning rage at the injustice of what was happening to him, and to me. A rage that lashed out at everything, even God, for letting him suffer this way. Without a conscious effort, I unclasped my fingers and pulled my hands from under his body. I rose from the ground like a beast from the innards of the earth, leaves and strands of grass falling from me at the fury of sudden movement. I stood defiantly against the night, my arms stretched down and slightly behind me, the fingers of my hands curled into claws, the nails biting into the plash of my palm. But the pain was lost somewhere in the swirl of anger. I stared unblinkingly at the stars shining between steadily thickening clouds. Perhaps through the changing vista of the sky, I could gaze upon God.

A scream escaped from somewhere deep inside me, into the night, the sound filled with pain and something else. Something indescribable, but close to what I heard in the shrieks of those night birds.

Spent, I fell once more to my knees beside him. His eyes were closed now. My anger melted into fear as I looked at him. He seemed dead, and then I noticed the slight rise and fall of his chest. I took his hand. The palm was cold, but he opened his eyes at my touch. His eyes were filled with the pain of the death that was slowly taking him and the shock of not understanding what was happening to him.

"*Dim,*" I called him softly; the word slurred by held back sobs.

Deep silence engulfed us. Could he be dead with his eyes open, his chest rising and falling slightly in the darkness?

"*Dim.*"

He sighed.

That was enough. He was alive.

"We have to go....the cold."

He nodded, making a feeble attempt to move, to rise from the earth and shake away the shame of being reduced to something less than a man.

"I am sorry," he said after sometime.

"Please, *dim,* do not say that.' I begged not knowing what else to tell him.

"I am sorry," he said again, closing his eyes.

"I know."

The silence descended again. I waited, but not for much longer. The night was getting colder, his life was ebbing away.

"*Dim*," I called him.

His eyes flicked open.

"We have to go on. We can't give up now."

He closed his eyes, and then nodded after sometime.

I dug my hands under him and lifted him into a sitting position. All the muscles in my body ached from the effort. I wondered how much longer I could draw on the well of strength that was rapidly running dry. I had tried to be as gentle as I could, but with the strain and tension, I knew I caused him pain with each movement. I stopped for several seconds to catch my breath, gulping in cold air that scraped my already tortured lungs. The cold was oddly invigorating, replacing so little strength, where so much was lost.

I moved around him, taking a position behind him.

"*Dim*," I called him.

I detected a slight movement of his head.

"I am going to help you stand."

He nodded, more obviously now than before.

"It will be painful."

He took sometime before he nodded this time. He was considering the pain.

I dug my knees into the soft earth with the muscle in my arms and my back stretching, straining, aching, I lifted him. I felt him kick his legs in a feeble attempt to lend a hand, and we were both off the ground. I pushed him upright and held him. He swayed dangerously, but I held him. I wanted to shout, to scream into the night once more, but this time not in pain or fear, but in the certain knowledge that I just won a battle. If Ukela would die, it would not be here in the embrace of the dark night, among unfriendly shadows and malevolent night birds.

*   *   *   *

Ukela deserved more than the death of an animal of the wild. He was the best man a woman could have, at least had been when I married him. Our life, though not perfect, had been ideal till the day I sat shivering before the white woman doctor at the health center in the next village. I had never been sickly, not even as a child, so I did not take the nagging ache in my head as much other than stress. It could only have come from working long hours at the primary school where I taught pupils then going straight to the farm to tend to the crops. Perhaps it was from too much worrying how to improve the performance of the pupils, who seemed at every opportunity to fail all the subjects.

Ukela had not been there for me talk to. He was in the city where he worked. He only came back one weekend in two weeks. Though not happy with the arrangement, his job with the bank had been a dream come true, so I had to endure till he was able to arrange for me to join him in the big city. I was able to endure it because I knew it was hard on him too. At least he told me so each time he came home.

A little rest would take care of the ache in my head. I took permission from the headmistress and did not go to school or the farm for a whole week. Even that did not stop the dull throbbing ache that left me with the feeling that my heart was now in my head. Neither did it stop the strange shivers that gripped me at night while I slept, and the certain feeling that something was not right.

I only went to the health center after I discovered I could not sleep at night. Sitting before the makeshift table in the pristine office that smelled of drugs and ether, looking at a *Medicine Sans Frontier* poster on the wall behind the chair, trying to remember the answers to the doctor's questions, I wondered what I was doing here. Her voice was soft and gentle, but insistent as she tried to make me remember how long the aches, the shivers and the fear had been there. She made notes as we talked. She looked into my eyes, peeling back the lids, shook her head at the reading from the thermometer stuck under my armpit and did all the things doctors did in hospitals. I left some time later with some drugs in my purse, and hanging behind me in the office, a promise to come back in two weeks, or when I felt the symptoms get worse. I knew they would go away as soon as I started taking drugs. I also left behind half a syringe of blood for the tests she wanted.

Needless to say, I did not go back for two weeks. The drugs worked wonders, and in a few days I was feeling as strong as I needed to. I went back just to let her know I was all right. She welcomed me with a smile, but I could see the hint of a troubled look. I wondered briefly what bothered her. She asked how I felt and tried to make small talk, but I sensed she was holding back on the things she really wanted to say.

"You are married," she asked suddenly after some time.

I nodded. "Yes," I said, my eyes straying to the single gold band around my finger as if in confirmation that it was still there.

"Where is your husband?"

"Oh, he works with a bank in the city," I told her, glad to talk about something else besides aches, pains and drugs.

"How long have you been married?"

"Not so long. Four years."

"Do you have children?"

I turned away, an involuntary reaction to an innocent question that brought back painful memories of being childless; the mocking stares that seemed to say it was all your fault, and worse, perhaps something terrible was wrong with you.

"I am sorry," she said, catching the look.

I shook my head slowly. "We do not have a child, yet."

"I am sorry," she repeated. "Do you love your husband?"

I nodded. "Yes, very much."

"Can you ask him to come? I need to talk with him."

I looked at her for a long time before I nodded. "Yes, I can ask him to come."

Another long look.

"I hope all is well with me?"

She smiled this time, nodding. "Yes. Just take your drugs and you will be all right."

"When do you want to see Ukela?"

"Ukela?" she asked, pronouncing the name as if she tried to talk with water between her teeth.

"My husband, he is Ukela."

"Okay." she said and smiled. "You can come anytime he is around. The sooner is better for me."

I thanked her as she walked with me to the door of her office. She stood with me, tried to smile, but her eyes were serious. She took my hand in both of hers. Her hands were cool but not cold, her touch gentle. She looked into my eyes.

"You will be okay," she told me.

I nodded not knowing why I found it very difficult to believe her. Perhaps it was something I felt deep inside where no thermometers or drugs could touch. After she let go of my hands and stood in the doorway to watch me go, I walked away towards the other door.

It was not difficult getting Ukela to come. It was harder telling him a story without an end. Yes, the white woman doctor in Obeta wanted to see him, but no I did not know why. I had only gone to see her because I felt ill, but now I am better. Confused as I was, and wondering what this was all about, he agreed to go with me.

Sitting before the doctor's desk felt uncannily like being before the village chief priest, not knowing why you are there or what the gods of the land would say. In her calm, soothing voice, she welcomed Ukela. She asked questions. Strange questions.

Had he been feeling sick recently? Perhaps a headache?

Yes.

For how long?

He could not remember.
How about diarrhea?
Yes
Night fever?
Yes.

She made notes, the same way she did when she spoke with me. She would look straight at Ukela, right between the eyes as he spoke, then she would make notes, taking her eyes off his face only to look at the paper.

Though she smiled, she looked serious and concerned. She would like to draw a little of his blood for a test. She hoped he would not mind. Too confused to mind, Ukela pulled up the left sleeve of his shirt and watched in silence as she pushed the needle into his vein. The blood surged into the plunger, filling it. She pulled the needle out and placed an alcohol soaked swab on the tiny blob of blood.

We went back the next day.

She sat behind the desk looking at us.

"Welcome."

Ukela muttered thanks. I only nodded, too apprehensive to speak.

"You are both very ill," she said suddenly, softly.

"Very ill?" Ukela asked, repeating what she said like a child slow in thought. He turned to look at me; his eyes seeking a comprehension, an understanding of what the doctor said.

Looking back at that day now, perhaps there had also been some guilt in his eyes that I refused to see. Then, I had chosen to see only the need to know. I reached out and took his hand under the desk.

"Yes."

"What is the problem with us?" I asked.

"I want you to know this is something we can manage," the doctor said evasively.

"Manage?" Once more, it was Ukela, sounding like a retarded child. The doctor nodded. "At this stage, we can slow down the progress of the illness. You can live normal lives."

"Slow down the progress of the illness?" Ukela asked.

I wanted to tell him to shut up, but did not. I never did. Instead I turned to the doctor.

"What is this all this about?" I asked, feeling a sudden trace of anger. My voice was tight, terse.

She looked at me with so much understanding in her eyes I almost started crying.

"I don't know how else to tell you this, but you have the virus."

"What virus?" Ukela asked.

"The HIV virus, that causes AIDS."

I had tried to believe she was not talking about the death that killed the body and the soul. But the name of the dreaded disease was a certain death knell. It hung in the air long after she stopped talking.

A roar filled my ears. I heard Ukela's voice from the end of a deep tunnel, rebounding off walls and washing over me like cold water. I felt a sharp pain lance through my heart. I felt something heavy on my shoulder, and turned to look at it through eyes clouded with nausea. The doctor stood beside me. Her hand was on my shoulder, the kindness of the gesture lost in the maze of pain and confusion into which her words plunged me.

I turned to look at Ukela.

He just sat there staring at me. He was as stunned as I was, perhaps worse.

"Ukela?" I called out to him.

He started shaking his head, as if in denial of something, perhaps a silent accusation he heard in my voice, but stopped. His mouth opened, as if to continue the denial, but closed.

"Ukela?" I called him again.

"Take it easy," the doctor said. "You need to talk about this alone."

We talked about it. Ukela sat on the bed, and I sat on the small kitchen table facing him. We looked at each other. I made no attempt to hide the pain and the anger I felt at what I had already realized was betrayal.

He watched me, his eyes wary, his fear infectious.

"Ukela?"

That name became all the questions I wanted to ask him. Perhaps all the accusation.

"Mame please, I can explain this," he said.

"You can explain it?" I asked, working so terribly hard at stopping myself from screaming.

He just sat there staring at me, looking so small.

"Go ahead, explain it Ukela. Explain how you just destroyed my life. Our life."

I had not wanted to cry, but I felt sudden hot tears running down my cheeks. I could not hold back any longer the pain, the shame, the fear and the certain knowledge that my life had been too suddenly cut short by something I did not know, something I was not part of.

At first he did not know what to do. His hesitation crawled across the space between us like a tentative little monster, seeking to comfort but also irritating at the same time. I felt him move when he stood up and stopped before me. Then I was in his arms. I wanted to push him away, filled with instant revulsion, but life, the love we had shared for so long, took over me.

It had been another woman in the big city, and he had been lonely. I listened quietly, wondering where I had gone wrong, what I had done wrong. I had given him the best of me there was, and all I got back was this, a shortening of my life. Even what was left of it would be filled with pain. No matter how much I tried to hate him, I found I could not. I hated what he did, but not him. I had loved him when there was no reason to. Could I desert him now we needed each other?

Not even when they came to tell me he could not die among his own. They had been afraid his presence would not only bring down the wrath of the gods on them, but would also spread the virus that killed the body and soul. My pleas, my explanations that his presence was not a threat to anyone, were met with stony stares full of fear and uncertainty. They wanted him to go away, to disappear not just from their lives, but from the face of the earth. Then I knew I had to take Ukela away. Far away from their withering scorn, their mockery, from the look in their eyes that told me he was much lower than a human being. In reducing him to that level of existence, they had reduced me too. I had to give him a chance to go in what little peace he could find.

I swung a kick at the door of the hut, which opened with a loud creaking sound. Everything creaked tonight. I could not find oil for the hinges when I came to clean the place the day before. I did not bother. It was only a place for the dying and the dead. The dying and the dead knew no beauty. No one had been here since after his mother died. I had spent hours cleaning the hut, but a faint smell of dust still hung in the air, a reminder of the inevitability of degeneration and decay. The darkness inside was thick, palpable and felt immovably liquid. There were no shadows. Just thick unmoving blackness.

I got him to the bed without falling over anything. Lowering him onto the thin mattress felt like having a heavy burden off my spirit. I sat on the bed beside him, taking deep breaths to calm the flutter of my heart. I closed my eyes to the dull ache that had started again in my head. His touch, the dry caress of his finger forced my eyes open. He was trying to touch me in the darkness. I took his hand in both of mine, squeezing gently. It felt so cold and lifeless. I felt his eyes on me and even in the unyielding darkness knew they were gazing at me.

"I will die," he said softly.

"No *dim*," I protested weakly, "the doctor said..."

He laughed quietly at that, the sound seeming to come from not just inside but around him.

"I know what the doctor said," he told me, pausing for breath. "I know what I know."

"What do you know *dim*?"

"I have lost my laughter."

"Your laughter?" I asked knowing what he meant. Among my people laughter can represent so many things–happiness, joy, even life itself. In this case, I knew he meant all of these.

"Yes, behind those hills."

Behind those hills was the road to the city, where he was infected.

I squeezed his hands.

"No *dim*, your laughter is here. Not lost behind those hills. You will be alright."

I heard the sound of his head moving on the mattress, and without seeing the movement, knew he was shaking it in a no.

"I cannot even die among my own." He whispered, his voice loaded equally with pain and anger. "I cannot die in peace."

"You are among your own. You are with me."

He nodded. The movement of his head was much stronger than before. His eyes seemed to shine in the darkness, so much that I could see them as much as feel them. There was something in them I could not understand.

"Yes. I know."

"You do?"

"Yes," he breathed.

"The pain will go, soon."

He nodded again, his eyes closed.

His head had moved with such certainty, that I had a sudden premonition he was not agreeing to what I just told him, but something he either believed or knew, something more profound and deeper than the comfort my words could give or his pain could take away.

This thought was so strong, so disturbing I was scared instead of hoping. When he opened his eyes, the pain was gone. His gaze was calm and filled with that look I could not understand. Even his voice had changed. It was no longer hoarse and tortured, but soft and clear, like the song of the Kingfisher beside a stream.

"Yes *dim*," I was overwhelmed by the sudden change in him, yet tried not to hope for too much.

Among my people, it was believed that final peace came to all who would die, just before they drew their last breath.

"I am sorry."

"No..."

He raised his free hand, stopping me.

"I am sorry for the pain, the shame..." he stopped.

He was silent for several seconds.

"My laughter is here...with you."

"Yes *dim*, yes."

"Pray with me," he said suddenly. "Close your eyes and pray with me."

I almost screamed with joy. Ukela had not asked me to pray with him since the sickness took over our lives. Until now. He had found it difficult to believe in a God that allowed his pain, his agony.

I took his other hand too, clasping both of them between mine. I closed my eyes, but felt him watching me. I knew he would close his eyes too. I waited, listening to the gentle sound of his breath, for him to tell me what he wanted me to pray for.

"Goodbye my love," he said, his voice so soft and so low I almost did not hear him.

I felt his hands go slack and slip away from mine. I opened my eyes. His eyes were still open, but stared vacantly beyond me at the space above. The slow rise and fall of his chest had stopped. I did not need to touch him to know he was dead. I stared at Ukela for a long time, not knowing what to do. The death that killed him took so long it had robbed me even of sorrow. I only felt sapped, empty, denied. But I also felt an odd joy that pain, agony could no longer touch him. At least not here on earth.

I had thought of this moment. I thought I would scream into the night when he died. Yes, somehow, I had known he would die at night. It seemed so appropriate. I had believed I would scream my defiance at the face of the death that killed him. As I let my gaze rove his face, I realized I did not even have the strength to cry. I could only feel happy for his release, and waited for my turn with the darkness.

I reached out and took his hand, the way I did when he was alive.

"Goodbye *dim*," I told him.

As I rose from the bed, I heard his last words about our laughter: "My laughter is here...with you." He had lied and told the truth at the same time. My laughter had died with him, but his would remain with me till the darkness also took me.

I looked around the hut for the last time, then at him on the bed. He seemed to glow. I could see him as clearly as if a light was in the room. I smiled, knowing I saw him in my mind. I turned away and walked towards the door.

Outside, the sound of the night had stopped. Only a soft breeze sighed mournfully through the trees, as if even nature knew my loss. I stopped at the doorway and turned to look at him lying on the bed for last time, then stepped out into the night.

My laughter is here...with you.

AIDS Elegy (1981-2006)

Becky Thompson

It is the day when

> tight buns whistle on Castro Street
> church bells ringing Harvey Milk's tune

> young men stand in line for tests
> not yet invented

> Haitians run from Papa Doc and cameras
> prostitutes count condoms in alley ways

It is the day when

> Rock Hudson admits Doris Day is a doll
> Magic gives up b-ball

> black men in door ways love
> black men in choir boxes

African children cradle mothers
AZT an elixir coded in white

It is the day when

infections passed in love
replace loving during pass laws

Angels in America turn to
black women in the shadows

the virus twirls around itself
mutating an unimaginable frenzy

Twenty five comes and we still keep counting

This Man (and His Hound)*

Joop Bersee

This man is made out of stone,
granite of your broken sink.
He makes sure that no one can
close the door called AIDS. His
shoe-shine-shoe keeps the door ajar.
He enjoys being watched as he
reads his books with fairy tales.
He believes in plants and flowers;
they make the dead people smile,
they change the flow of rivers,

change what is north into south.
But it doesn't change the night.
It doesn't change the appetite
of the dead animals, of
the gnawing on fingers, the
face of the one you will never
meet again. He sows dead seed.
The harvest overwhelming.

He must be all smile and wealth;
shoe-shine-shoe keeps the door ajar.

Plants and veins grow and rot,
grow and rot, air the assassin,
soil, and a black horse eating
meat. His dead sleep like the fast
moving clouds, the small lizards
waiting for a bit of sun.
It takes as long as it takes.
Hiding underneath a big
boulder, waiting for raindrops
and their little flies of spring.

*South African President Thabo Mbeki and his minister of Hell-th.

HIV Needs Assessment

Roy Jacobstein

Everywhere the faces, hair, limbs
    are coal, obsidian, flawless black
        sapphire, thus the rare *mzungu**

like me stands out the way those
    remaining white moths once did
        on industrialized London's trees.

A month fluttering *The Warm Heart*
    of Africa's long length on this *Needs*
        Assessment. We've found the needs

many. But let us not talk of that,
    as the people do not. Focus instead
        on the vivid oleander & limpid sky

that domes the arid volcanic hills,
    its lapis mirrored in the uniforms
        of the file of schoolgirls who stride

the side of the road. And when the talk,
        matter-of-fact, beyond resigned, bears
                left at the roundabout, glances upon

a cousin's funeral attended yesterday,
        the two added children your colleague
                from Lilongwe is now raising alone,

funeral venues for this weekend, just
        sit there as the *Project Vehicle* propels
                you onward to the next *Site*, past

the lone ads for toothpaste
        & for study opportunity abroad,
                & the many for caskets ("lightweight,

can be carried by one"), & say nothing.

*Swahili for "white person" (literally, "to travel around")

The Storm's Eye

Ebony Golden

what to think of mortality
        corner store flashes
        glass bottle souls   pebbled knees
           baby spirits that never squeezed
        warmth from mother's breasts a vulnerable shaking leaf
        scathing heat that brews and brews
        charred aftershock   remarkable destiny
life juice wrung from solitude's pale pallet

her body begs the question
        a fertile limb
        slick jade leaf sprout earth slurps
        ginger nectar affinity
        purple glowing pirouettes
she does not digest such a passing

how lungs form goodbye
        in asthmatic bursts
        memory heaves that (re)collect

the blisters like erupting volcano
and homemade salve to cool the magma swallows

how lungs from goodbye
       maybe in grown woman lullaby
       like *amazing grace* snagged from aretha's honey bosoms
       or some throaty chaka khan utterance
             (i rocked your skin and bone frame
             as *my funny valentine* swooned
             around us in a sage smoked bedroom)

how to forgive trips never taken
       leave a path of postcards orbiting grave
       and tiny cups of india's spice next to lilies
       hum swahili river songs when i cry of you
       and teach your daughters to count to 50 in tagalog
       leave split coconut at your dirt altar
       instruct your son never to stir in pots with knives
we will fly
dig our heals in pyramid sand
       dance in brazilian arms
even in our dreams

how to avoid goodbye
       the words do not manifest
       are weightless waterless phantom
             like ether you are simply vapor now
                    coffee sweetener
                    warming quilts
                    perfect driving music
the tangerine breeze
 i love matterlessly

To the Young Warriors

Chanell Harris

for Rae Louis Thornton

I wouldn't think
living with AIDS so long
would make you change
your mind
about how devastating
the disease is.
You acted invincible,
told us all the necessary
statistics, like you still had sex
with your husband
because of the low percentage
of female to male
transmission.
In trying to convince
yourself, you
made it normal, regular, doable.
Even in telling
us your past
you made it

"not my fault."
Trying to teach
tolerance, awareness
you taught that it was beatable.
You said that abstinence
was a "good idea"
when for you it was a matter
of life and death.
You didn't use your fury
to change young lives
and at 14 I knew
what we needed to hear.
I didn't forgive you.
You said, "I'm Okay."
I didn't believe your lies.

Tallies and Tolls

Melanie Henderson

numbers never held
so much pain and loss
at the realization that to some,

you're only human if your body is
a self-sufficient, self-healing
war machine

even when it's under attack
from all fronts
every border menacing,

testing your vermillion heart
and all you want to do is
wave the white flag

yet combat continues
and most machines do fail when

left

                              alone

          staggering

vulnerable to agents
who sully your white flags
with paintball guns,

piercing your humanity,
tears fall down your fragile face
covered with bluing skin

dropping you to the ground
eyes locked on the sky,
waiting for God.

you
the newest victim
of the serial acronym

I hold both your hands
as you succumb
to the battlefield of breathing

The Rose and the Hummingbird

Diane Harriford

Between us, we'd had sex with most of the world. I started in Sioux City, Iowa in the playground of Hopkins School demanding that Carl, James and Dennis show it to me. After that, it just got better and better. There was my high school friend Linda, who lived on a farm where we practiced sex and drank beer and then there were the guys stationed at the air force base: Sweet Pea from the Bronx, Bobby the Puerto Rican, and Richard, the love of my young life. These sexual adventures lasted well into my 30s.

While I was doing that part of the world, Peter, who was born in England and spent his adolescence in Australia and was a bit younger, was just getting himself together. He began charming old men in high school to get away from his drunken father and after graduating, followed them to Athens, London and Amsterdam. He finally ended up in New York where he kicked the drug and alcohol habit that he had picked up along the way. He was doing temp work at a publishing house where we met and began to talk.

It was only later that I realized that his interest in me was in part due to his belief that I looked like Sugar Ray Leonard who he found attractive. I had never met anyone from Australia. His blue eyes, strong arms, and charm were hard to resist. As a recovering alcoholic, he would talk openly and honestly about his past life and I felt I could do the same. We had learned to do sex quite well, but intimacy had not been in our repertoire. Together we did both. We worried about HIV from the beginning, yet we quickly decided that we were too beautiful, too special to let it catch up with us. Our love would ward off danger.

I loved Peter because he did the laundry and listened to the opera on Saturday afternoons. I often said the only reason he stayed with me was so that he could enjoy my mother's superb cooking once a year since I had no interest in cooking and neither did he. He was a very good housewife in every way, which pleased my mother who hoped it might rub off on me. Peter and I also had special games. Because he never liked to spend money on himself, he'd make lists of things he wanted and put it where I could see it. Then I would go buy them. He'd say, "You shouldn't have, I'll take it back," but the presents never left the apartment. I loved to go to bars and have him come over and pick me up and take me home as though we were strangers having sex for the first time.

The next years were great years, the kind that special people had. I had finally finished my PhD and Peter got through college and medical school more easily than either of us would have ever imagined. As two people who had been so alone in the world before finding each other, we both knew that we could have accomplished neither the PhD nor the MD without each other. I made most of the money to support us during this time, as we scrimped to make the arrangement work. I was tickled at the thought of being the doctor's wife and even more tickled that Peter was going to be the doctor. Peter also took enormous pleasure from his relationship with his younger brother Raymond. As children, Peter had always been

Raymond's protector, and felt guilty when Raymond followed him into alcohol and drug addiction. Raymond's move to the United States and subsequent sobriety made Peter happy.

We often talked about what the future would look like, the plan: he would be an emergency room doctor working on weekends while I could quit being an academic, which didn't seem to suit my large personality and need to play. Peter was my playmate. The one toy he promised me was a blue Mercedes convertible, custom made. Peter could not think about what he wanted with this new status. But one Christmas after I bought him a new Electrolux vacuum cleaner, we began to visit the Sharper Image store regularly and fantasized about all the great home appliance gadgets he would buy. Of course, we planned to continue to travel as we did each year. Now, we would travel in style rather than in the hostels where we often stayed.

After eight years together, the first worst moment was when I came home from work in 1989 and Peter told me he was HIV positive. Peter was less than a month from graduating from medical school. For his graduation party, about ten close friends came, all of whom by then had learned of the diagnosis. An event we had planned for so long seemed to be entirely beside the point.

The next worst moment was when our dear friends invited us to dinner shortly after hearing Peter's diagnosis. Our hostess told us very sincerely how she knew people with an HIV status were not pariahs. But then we noticed that Peter was given his own private plate of appetizers, while the rest of us shared. We were speechless. Peter could not eat and our hostess was unable to understand his sudden loss of appetite.

For the next four years, we did everything we could to avoid further worst moments. I became an AIDS expert chasing down every new treatment imaginable. We monitored Peter's eating and sleeping and believed we could beat his getting sicker, hoping that there would be a cure, or at least a vaccine soon. We traveled to

Mexico, Florida, and all through the Caribbean, managing to live it up while Peter first did his residency and then worked part time in an emergency room. Each summer we rented a house on the Cape and were joined by an ever-eclectic group of friends. We felt we were running ahead of a speeding train and Peter's T cells were holding at 250, where they were when he was first diagnosed.

The next worst moment was when, in 1993, while working in a hospital, he contracted pneumonia that landed him in a hospital as a patient for five weeks. He was never really the same after that. We had to acknowledge that he was sick. The next worst moment was a few months later when we took a cab all the way from 107th Street to 54th Street and 5th Avenue to St. Thomas Episcopal Church to hear his favorite, Jessye Norman. As we entered, I could see people assuming I was his caretaker. He looked like he was dying. I felt a disconnect that only dying gives you.

The next worst moment was two weeks later when we went to a doctor's appointment. Peter, Raymond and I went to all of his doctor's appointments together. We felt that we all needed to hear what the doctor said since we could not count on just one or two of us to take in the information. This time, we had gone because Peter seemed to be falling asleep in the middle of meals and other times when he should have been awake. Sometimes he would forget where he was going and he was losing weight. We thought he should get off AZT or get testosterone shots. We decided before we left that he had something manageable. When we got to the doctor, after an exhaustive exam, the doctor said he had PML, a condition in which the myelin sheaves, the wrappings on the nerve cells in the brain, would harden and cause paralysis in different places in his body. At that moment, he was given a death sentence but one where we would not know when death would strike. Would he be paralyzed? Would he lose the use of his legs? Would he lose his speech? Would he go blind? Would he have dementia? I remember thinking that at least he wasn't going to be bald headed. He had beautiful curly hair, a full head of hair that had always pleased him.

The worst moment *wasn't* that Saturday on Memorial Day weekend when Peter finally died. On Thursday afternoon, Peter went into a coma. While he was in the coma, I had called everyone: my therapist who was vacationing in Ireland, doctor friends, his brother and many others. People began gathering that Thursday evening and stayed up all night, assuming that he would be going at any moment. I had promised him I would be with him when he died. He didn't die Thursday. Finally, people left.

At 2:00 on Friday afternoon, Peter awakened from the coma to announce that we needed to get him a baked potato immediately. For the last several months, his diet had consisted of baked potatoes, ice cream, any kind of chocolate and tea. Before his caretaker could make it to the kitchen to fix him a potato, he began demanding that this six foot, two hundred and fifty pound woman, who he had often referred to as "a beast" tell him whether she was a man or a woman. She shook her head and went in search of the potato. She, like the rest of us, was happy to see he was still with us. Peter began shouting at his brother to leave and go to work saying, "You're a lay about who won't amount to anything. Why are you here? Why aren't you at work?"

As much as we had already witnessed Peter's dementia, it still surprised us to hear him speak that way. The Peter we had known was unfailingly polite, religiously a member of the English working class (neither snobby nor rude, predictably civil). Eventually his brother and the caretaker left, and I lay down beside him, knowing that would calm him. He rubbed my outer thigh as he had done for years, marveling, as though it was the first time, at how smooth and soft my skin felt to him. Then, he went to sleep around 8:00 that evening. I went into the other room to get some sleep. I woke up at 3:00, worried he was alone, and went to lie with him again.

Once I entered the room, I realized he was dying, that his spirit was on the ceiling. I called his brother who thought I was nuts (with my talking about a spirit on a ceiling) but we were both nuts already. I told him if he wanted to say anything more to Peter, this was the time. Peter always said that people die in the morning and now I knew what he meant. Raymond came over quickly and I left to get the newspaper and have breakfast. I came back within a couple of hours and his spirit was still on the ceiling. By this time, the caretaker, the acupuncturist, and the masseuse had come. He was back in a coma; his spirit hovering and I realized I could not stay to watch. I left, returned at 4:00 and he was still in a coma. I said, "You must go now. We can't win. We fought as hard as we can. You have to go. I know I told you I would be with you when you died and I am back. So you can go." As I spoke to him, I wasn't sure whether I could rely upon spoken language anymore to assure him I was there. So, I decided to put Jessye Norman on, his favorite aria. I sat on the bed next to him and listened with him. Two minutes into her aria, I heard his breathing stop, a rattle escaped from his throat; the blood seemed to drain from his body.

The caretaker came in and I insisted that she wash him, clean his fingernails, wash his hair, and dress him in his full length purple kimono that he wore around the house. I was busy looking for ID cards, mementos from his life on earth, which I taped to his body. I remember thinking that wherever he goes, people might not know who he is or his identity might be mistaken. With ID cards and pictures of us, pictures of his brother, pictures of our dog taped to his body, he could remember who he was even if others could not. I remember thinking what I was doing was perfectly sane. I kept thinking, you know Peter, he might go somewhere and get befuddled, forget who he is, and that I would not be there to remind him. It is so strange, how the mind works, thinking what I was doing was perfectly normal, thinking I could have some influence over him in his next place he went. It was only some months later, talking to anthropologist friends that I learned that these death rituals happened in most cultures. I guess I was in touch with something old and deep.

The moment after Peter rattled, I finally knew he was dead when a breeze blew through the room and carried his spirit with it. There was something about that awareness that connected me, that helped me know that his death was not the worst moment in our lives. In death, we were connected in ways we could not be connected in life. Sometimes I still feel his spirit in the breeze.

For Robby

Anna Forbes

*and even if we are occupied with important things, and even if
we attain honor or fall into misfortune, still let us remember how
good it was once here, where we were all together, united by a
good and kind feeling which made us... better perhaps than we
are.*

—Fyodor Dostoevsky, from *The Brothers Karamazov*

My bedridden brother
How I will miss you
When your days are accomplished
And you can move on

I sit by your bedside
These long winter evenings
Some pain and some boredom
Weave through our talk

Your sad, wasting body
Our external focus
But in reaching for your heart
I'm strengthening mine

The six years I've known you
You've always insisted
That people are better
Than even they know

And here in your illness
Is my object lesson
Because you believe it
In your room, we are.

SECTION IV

We, the Meeting of Twin Edges, the Same Blood

Who Decided

Lamont B. Steptoe

who decided aids
would be the plague

who decided to visit
upon the 20th and 21st centuries
a nightmare a global pandemic?

who decided
to assassinate millions
over burden graveyards
with youth and beauty and truth?

who decided Blacks and Latinos
gays and other colored folks
of the planet should fall victim
to their passions
babies should spoil
in the canning jars of wombs?
who decided to implement

such evil in our time?
who decided to commit such a crime?
who decided this?

A River in Africa

Truth Thomas

4 Vie

Being black in Africa, and HIV positive, is no longer a shocking matter. It has become as commonplace as the flu, only deadlier. Although they comprise only 10 percent of the world's population, Africans constitute more than 60 percent of the AIDS-infected population. As a result of colonialization, healthcare spending for Africans in Africa has historically been inadequate, leaving a legacy of high mortality in many regions. Much more HIV/AIDS related education is needed in Africa since no policy or law alone can combat this HIV/AIDS related discrimination. Many governments in sub-Saharan Africa denied that there was a problem for years, and are only now starting to work towards solutions. Without a unified plan of action, cemeteries will swell with the dead.

****

Being black in America, and HIV positive, is no longer a shocking matter. It has become as commonplace as the flu, only deadlier. Although they comprise only 12 percent of the US population, African Americans constitute more than 50 percent of the AIDS-infected population. As a result of racism, healthcare spending for Africans in America has historically been inadequate, leaving a legacy of high mortality in many regions. Much more HIV/AIDS related education is needed in America since no policy or law alone can combat this HIV/AIDS related discrimination. Many politicians in the United States government denied that there was a problem for years, and are only now starting to work towards solutions. Without a unified plan of action, cemeteries will swell with the dead.

The Vilification of Peter Mwai:
A Story of Fear and Racism

L. E. Scott

In 1976, I was living and working in London, England and while there I met people from all over the world, some of who were from Aotearoa/New Zealand. I knew roughly where on the planet this was and that, contrary to a common misconception, it was not a part of Australia, but little else.

White New Zealanders I met often told me their country was a multicultural society that worked equally for all and that there was no racism between white New Zealanders and the indigenous people of color, the Maori. As an African American who had traveled to various parts of the world, I was well aware that where there were white people and people of color living together, racism lived. So I was curious about Aotearoa/New Zealand. In 1976, I traveled to Wellington, the capital city. If I needed further proof that black and white people do not live in the same reality when it comes to racism, I found it in Aotearoa/New Zealand.

Shortly after arriving I was living through what became known as the "dawn raids." Police and immigration officials would arrive at homes in the very early morning looking for "overstayers"—immigrants whose visas or work permits had expired. Sometimes the officials knocked, sometimes they kicked the door down. It became clear that the profile of an overstayer was "someone who doesn't look like us." Ignoring the reality that New Zealanders were both brown and white and that there were plenty of white immigrants, the "someone" in the equation was brown and the "us" was white. With the downturn in the economy in the late 1970s, the people of color from Pacific Island countries such as Fiji, Samoa and Tonga who had been encouraged to come to Aotearoa/New Zealand to work in the factories and car-plants were no longer needed for their cheap labor.

The overt racism of the dawn raids did not occur in a vacuum. Aotearoa/New Zealand is a country that was "discovered" and subsequently colonized by white people about 200 years ago. That process involved the subjugation and dehumanization of the indigenous people, the Maori. White people stole Maori tribal lands; tried to destroy their laws, customs, social structures, and language; and damaged their cultural beliefs. White people spread diseases that decimated the Maori population.

While Aotearoa/New Zealand has worked hard in recent times to create the illusion of a country of racial harmony and equal opportunity, all the statistics reveal the lie: Maori health is worse than that of pakeha (the name Maori gave to white people), Maori die ten years earlier than pakeha, the education system doesn't serve Maori well, Maori unemployment is high, poverty is a fact of Maori life, and Maori are hugely over-represented in the prison population. Notwithstanding this, Maori continue to wage the struggle to get their lands back or be compensated for their loss, and fight to keep their language alive, to improve the delivery of education, justice, and health to their people and to regain the control and means to shape their own destiny.

When the AIDS epidemic emerged twenty-five years ago, Aotearoa/New Zealand, because of its relative isolation, faced little early threat. Their isolation gave them a chance to learn from what was happening elsewhere and prepare itself for what would inevitably reach its shores. Unfortunately, the country didn't take full advantage of this and the ignorance, fear and misinformation seen worldwide were largely replicated.

HIV/AIDS is not a white or black disease, but poverty and racism certainly increases people's vulnerability worldwide. That reality has also been replicated in Aotearoa/New Zealand. Before the 1990s the African and African American population of Aotearoa/New Zealand was extremely small, but it grew considerably through that decade, drawn by study or work opportunities or from the refugee quotas accepted by the government. Most who came were Africans from Kenya, Uganda, Nigeria, Mali and Somalia and many were refugees. (New Zealand's 2001 Census listed 7,413 African and African American residents in a total population of 3,737,277.)[1] As the African community became more visible, so too did the racism of white New Zealanders towards its members.

In 1993, I was witness to events that exposed this running sore of racism in Aotearoa/New Zealand. I had just arrived back in Aotearoa/New Zealand from a holiday. As I walked into the kitchen to make myself a cup of coffee, a friend called, asking, "Have you heard?" I knew instantly that something was terribly wrong. Someone must be dead, hurt badly, or in deep trouble. My body tightened.

"Peter Mwai has been arrested," my friend said after a long pause. My mind turned to Peter Mwai, a young Kenyan musician, dancer and teacher living in Auckland (the largest city in Aotearoa/New Zealand), who from what I had seen wasn't someone who would get into serious trouble with the police. My friend told me that Peter Mwai had been arrested and charged under the Crimes Act with "knowingly spreading an infectious disease," in this case the HIV virus. The police had arrested Mwai after a 28-year-old woman laid a complaint alleging that she had had unprotected sex with him and subsequently discovered that he had infected her with the HIV virus.

In the Auckland District Court in October 1993, Mwai entered no plea and was remanded in custody while the police built their case against him. It was the first case in Aotearoa/New Zealand dealing with a person alleged to have had unprotected sex whilst knowing he was HIV-positive. As they proceeded, the police suggested that there might be other women at risk, so a nationwide alert was sent out advising that anyone who had "had sex with a Kenyan" should seek medical advice urgently. If any of these women tested HIV-positive they were to contact the police so it could be determined if the source of their infection could be traced back to Peter Mwai.[2]

All the major media outlets carried the story about Mwai, including the alert to other possible sexual partners, with some publishing a photograph of him. One newspaper ran a large head and shoulder photo of Mwai on the front page with the headline, "The Face of Fear," and the story went on to talk about the number of women who may have been "at risk from the Kenyan man."[3]

The media coverage of the case and its background added fuel to some ugly manifestations of human behavior. Photocopied pictures of Mwai appeared around Auckland with the caption, "Have you slept with this man?" and warned women who had had sex with him to contact one of the various agencies that were listed on the poster. The source of these posters was not known. The police and the New Zealand AIDS Foundation claimed they had nothing to do with them. Then, a letter was circulated around the Auckland University campus, originating from the university's Student Accommodation Office, stating that if any students had had "consensual or nonconsensual sex with Peter Mwai," they could get confidential help and counseling from telephone numbers listed in the letter. So now it was being suggested that not only was he spreading the HIV virus, he was out there raping women as well. It was also reported that the Director of the Auckland Sexual Health Service at that time, Dr. Janet Say, had warned New Zealanders to be particularly careful about having unprotected sex with visitors from high-risk countries. The same article went on to list several African countries in the grip of "heterosexual AIDS epidemics."[4]

The news media was really getting into its stride, telephoning Black people with a public profile and asking questions such as, "What do you think about the African man spreading the HIV virus? What stand is the African community taking in regard to Peter Mwai? What do you think when people say AIDS came from Africa?" The Black community as a whole did not bother to respond to these questions, other than to ask itself rhetorically whether, if the accused had been white, the media would have been asking the white community for its reaction to the behavior of one of its own.

What was very clear to the African and African American community in Aotearoa/New Zealand was that on the back of Peter Mwai being charged, the racists had come out in full dress. Black people were being asked by white people if they were from Kenya or if they knew Mwai and if it was "really true." It reached the point in Auckland that many Africans felt uncomfortable in public because strangers approached them in supermarkets, gas stations, on the street or in social situations. The tone and manner of the questioners was often ugly and offensive. And it didn't stop there. Some white people had a perversion of their own that they tried to transfer onto the sexuality of Black people and Africans who were married to or in relationships with white women. Many in the Black community were upset at being forced as a whole community to deal with the aftermath of Mwai being charged and meetings were held to try to deal with some of the misinformation and hysteria.

Peter Mwai was convicted in 1994 and sentenced to seven years' jail. Mwai was never allowed to be innocent—he was presumed guilty before his trial ever started and the media headlines helped to fan the flames of that injustice. This is not to say that Peter Mwai *was* innocent, simply that the atmosphere of fear, loathing and condemnation that prevailed in Aotearoa/New Zealand in relation to the case and its trial colored its outcome.

In early 1998, after nearly five years in prison and near death (Peter now was quite sick with AIDS) newspapers carried the story that Mwai was about to be released from prison and deported back to Africa and also that he had asked to be allowed to stay here for whatever little time he had left to live. Yvonne Martin, a reporter for *The Dominion* newspaper (now called *The Dominion Post*) wrote an article published on May 23, 1998, about Peter Mwai entitled "Evil on the loose."[5] The front-page promo for the article read: "Evil Peter Mwai–should this beast be let loose?" Ms. Martin informed readers that Peter Mwai might be released in September and that the activation of the removal order against him might be impeded by his poor health. The article also regurgitated the descriptions and comments that had fueled the fear and disgust five years earlier. She opened with, "He has been called the face of fear and a sexual predator" and went on to say that Peter Mwai was remembered as the AIDS man who inflicted the HIV virus on women he had sex with. The article quoted Mark Kaveney, the police officer who had headed the investigation, as saying that for the complainants' peace of mind Peter Mwai should "be on a plane" out of New Zealand. His "worst scenario" was that Mwai might not be accepted for travel by any airline because of ill health. So freely do we acquaint ourselves with the possibility of someone else's death.

Peter Mwai had gone through the justice system, been convicted, was serving his sentence and had a removal order against him awaiting his release. His deportation was to be dealt with in accordance with the policies and practices of the Immigration Department and the airlines. With this apparently straightforward application of the due process of law, what of value was left for the article to explore? It could have been a serious attempt to understand the human frailties that this case was so much about. It might have sought to provide some insight into who Peter Mwai was and the motivating forces of his life. Instead, Ms. Martin scratched around in the cold ashes of fear to poison public opinion regarding Mwai's pending release.

As this case unfolded, I saw not only the ignorance and racism of strangers but also the fear and animosity from white friends of the African community who turned against the community they had been so much a part of. Many of those friendships have never been rebuilt. Many Africans felt, with some justification, that the case was seen not just to concern an individual but to draw the entire African community under scrutiny. When the African Association of Auckland was asked to assist with Mwai's legal costs, the African community was divided in its reaction. Some felt that his right to legal representation and a fair trial should be supported whatever the charges, while others wanted to distance themselves as much as possible from the whole situation. Those divided views created considerable strain on relationships. It was painful to witness the African community paralysed with the fear of being painted with the same brush as "the African man spreading AIDS in Aotearoa/New Zealand." The hurt of that fear cuts deep in the soul.

In June 1998, Peter Mwai was released from prison. His request on compassionate grounds to be allowed to stay in this country was refused and he was deported to Kenya. A few months later, he died of AIDS-related illness.

References

1. Statistics Department, New Zealand, Census 2001 data.

2. *Sunday News* (Auckland, New Zealand), October 10, 1993, page 1, reporter Joseph Lose.

3. *Sunday News* (Auckland, New Zealand), October 17, 1993, page 1-2, reporter Joseph Lose.

4. *ibid.*

5. *The Dominion* (Wellington, New Zealand), May 23, 1998, page 17, reporter Yvonne Martin.

Terrorist

Alan King

for TW

you're soothed by
Cherokee myth that

ancestors wipe your
sweat on *labored nights*

when your body battles
an intruder

that won't withdraw
its troops

Timothy

Beth Synder

1.
Was the sky a Southwestern
casserole of cloud
and color, a purple in three shades, violet, maybe gray
one more layered taste
of Santa Fe
as he drove toward the ocher trees,
equipped for suicide:
pills and Scotch,
the passengers beside him?

2.
His was the far less vulgar place
of cookbooks, painting
candlesticks, a sound of flutes,
the wild sage
in a sweat lodge ring
so fierce with heat, the burning rock,
the bass of the Sioux warrior's drum,

where all relations,
all loves converge
and worldly desire
drops away
in ceremony.

3.
Was it relief
when he reached his way
past midnight unconsciousness?
This frail and tawny-haired boy,
a fellow who sensed the feminine
in all the fascinating forms
and now detached
from thirty-five years of history,
of ridicule and crippling HIV,
the lies of a German father who hid
being a Jew.

4.
Did the Catholic canon
help him at his end,
not the nuns who schooled him
with a narrow scope and scolding
nor the memories of a Mass or choir, Christmas Eve,
but did the magna mater,
did Mary, his favored, take his arm,
she who intercedes to give
the common man
the shelter of her cloak,
her clemency her consolation?
Did she paint him a breathtaking view?

5.
Iron the collar first,
he used to say.
It was Timothy
those January nights
in the bedroom by the halogen lamp,
crumpled shirt in hand,
starch can shaken,
with his half-smile, shy,
Let me show you one more time,
old friend.

I am free of all discomfort

Conditional Coming

M. L. Hunter

what if jesus christ
came back as a black man,
without my mothers' permission,
living with hiv

would you listen to me then?

Willie

Kimberly A. Collins

If Nzinga could
See her warriors she'd kick
their mocha asses

Shiny black
Marbles perched
On life's edge
Watching a kaleidoscope
Of agony

"Sis I got AIDS
I'm dying"

She knew
Pressing in
Kisses on flaccid
Cheeks that
once jumped
w/laughter
gone now

sunken in w/ hate
fallen between
Flesh

II
His cracked face
Told the story
Lost to her
Between cell blocks
Time lost
Doing time
Time lost
In a white Cyclops
Nightmare
Kneeling before
Him on concrete floors
Willie didn't get done
Did what had to be done
During lost time

III
Erasing time on
The outside
Driving needles
Through
Smooth black skin
Skin Big mama said was
Spooky blue
Willie tingling now on
The outside
Tuning out big Mama
& a high yellow mama
That didn't want

No black babies
Willie w/no milk
Searching for
his daddy's bottle
finding heroin instead

IV
Before bottles
Before needles
Sis was there
Born
4 days after him
To his father's sister
Them two
Thick as thieves
Nothin' but eyes peeking out
Under Big Mama's porch
Down south
Teasing her to tears
She wondered why
He was pretty black
w/ long eyelashes too

& sis wanted it back
Wanted to turn back
Run down south
Recover him
Grabbing his wet sheets
Tight
She wanted to pull him back

Tired now
Dirty needles

White women
He tried to loose
Himself in
Tired now
coming home
To love
He ran from
In disbelief
Running from
Children black like him
Running in white women
To erase him

V
Willie
Still runnin
He been runnin
& flyin'
Jumpin'
From his skin too long
Sis's love never
Eased his pain
Just made him honest

Willie been livin'
To die
Since he got here
"but who ain't"
He says
As the air leaves
Cheeks ballooned
w/laughter

Rose City Thorns

Yesod-Fredrick Douglas Knowles

Toto,
I still remember the way
you would tell me to lie flat on my back,
as if positioned for my very first sit-up.
You'd squeeze my tiny ankles,
ask me if I was *ready*
and catapult me into the air
as my tiny frame whirled
from a perfect release
into a full back flip;
massive head-rush
as I landed squarely on my feet, giggling,
pleading for another, then another, and another.

Rab,
I still remember the way
you stood outside the back stoop
leaned against the rusted, metal post
and watched me lace up.

I felt the pressure, even though I knew
I could beat my opponent, he was a wuss.
Still, my chest flamed.
I remember thinking to myself
that if I won the backyard grudge,
I would gain the honor of dating your daughter.
Now, nearly sixteen years later,
I see you glancing at me through my daughter's eyes.

Neicy,
I still remember the way
you would call weed, *fudama*.
You were the lone orator of a dead discourse.
I remember how I would sell you poison,
and watch you and my brother cook it,
smoke it, and feign for more.
I watched your youngest son, barely eight
run back and forth, desperately seeking his mother's attention
while the *strange man* who only came around twice a month
stole his lunch money from your hand.

Who could have comprehended your cries?
understood your fears as the virus infiltrated?

Old friends,
who believed it only consumed
fags and *junkies*, misunderstood you.
They isolated you, pointed their fingers
when you walked down the street;
sat for a drink, attempting to drown
infectious T cells,
conquering your kingdom.
Those friends didn't know shit.

They couldn't have possibly fathomed the casualties,
millions caught in the crossfire
of pharmaceutical warfare.

Your names no longer whisper in the dark.
Your memories are no longer phantoms
roaming empty hallways of hindrance
echoing anguish and isolation.
They're here, feeding me,
like ultraviolet light
nurturing wilted rose petals
dwindling into a thicket of thorns.

Satyr, Wounded

Stephen Mead

You remind me of that,
One of Michelangelo's kind
But smaller in frame, pain's
Thievery, the disease, taking,
Twisting muscles until
Only the eloquence of sleep
Realigns the pure curves,
The beautiful bones.

Mother Morphia also clears
Your plate, the eyes of bitter blue
Pale inside the tired crags
Returning warmth from some
Gibberish battle to your voice
Of whiskey.

I see old lovers in you, fallen warriors
All turned to the saints of tortured

Children, their tattoos & piercings
Clues to that fate there on white sheets.

Coming to we do not speak
Of the darker phase.
We give the wounds to amnesia,
The tears for Mom to release, necessary,
& love you any way with the bait
Of empathy.

You ask for a soda which I pass
To touch hands & there's a memory
For dance in the club of our blood,
You & I testimonies smiling
For our tribe's scriptures

Touch

Fred Joiner

before our ken
there was just stares
and bodies wasting

if only looks could heal

the work of their hands was holy
their ministry a sincere embrace—
a treatment without price

lamar

avery r. young

1991 ...
had to use thumpkin n pointy to wipe you off ...
poems sweatin over bedpost.
yo/name trapped
between spit or swallow.

i'se was real free fo/you.
so free ... my hands opened ... my arms rose ... my fall fell
love first in yo/funk of bootsy in middle of watts riot.

you said nothin bout bein
too weak
to speak
two weeks
be/fo i'se found out ...
me n Magic have somethin in common.

today ...
we keep our t cell-rian secret
folded
tucked
screamin.

Brown Sugar

Duriel Harris

I dream about you:
raw sugar eyes, skin,
hair, fading in waves
of spoiled water.
Black bubbles rise
from your lips,
sit hardening,
boils on the ocean's skim.
Your body fights
itself, pulling
at the seams,
splitting, gorged to spasm,
breaking to spume and spray.
You can't swim.

I am afraid for you
even though you assure me
you can take the world's shit
and spit it out.

Sixteen, Latin, Black,
queer manchild,
I want to warn you:
you are not the first.
History parts asscheeks
like a mythic sea,
It'll catch you
off guard, boy; take a limb,
a lung, your memory, your sleep.
Your memory.
Your sleep.

The BATA Dancer

Ayo Oyeku

Right in the scorching sun,
On the soft sand,
The *bata* dancer jumps—
Stimulating the mind of the spectators.

The drummer taps and slaps the animal skin.
The dancer lost in the gyration
Prances and darts around,
Displaying all sorts of acrobatics.

The spectators giggle with enthusiasm,
Translating the proverbial rhythms
Of the *bata* sound;
Praising, teaching and warning.

The dancer sprawls on,
Ignoring what the rhythms might be saying,
Ignoring what the night might bring,
Ignoring!

The Japanese Teahouse

Octavia McBride-Ahebee

to Greg Witcher

I can now see
the skirt hems of hants
stitched by the hands of the living
they keep with them in this sphere
the shame and vanity of us all
and so hide their naked spirits
in calico gowns shielding indigo slips
made loose for easy movement

La Fleur cannot see the ghosts of this house
vying for perfume and overripe papaya
spreading like yeast
in anticipation of bounty
spreading with the unyielding spell of raw cauliflower
He hears their whispers
entangled in the whistling overtones of searching mice
their frosted threats to lick
the healing fungus off the backs of caterpillars
and press into dust with their weightless humor

another cloak of his torment
-the anointed AZT-

Yet his third eye is sane, blighted
perceiving the lust of fear
flapping in its own daydreams
anxious to walk backwards
with those who die away from home

La Fleur wants to sleep with the cannons
near the vacant majesty of the Citadelle
under the guard of the grand Baron Samedi
in a grave that slides with no conscience
when the soil breathes too heavily
when forgotten things are collected
He wants to leave my city of foot-long sandwiches
and soft pretzels,
of trolley cars that triumph underneath the unbecoming frailty
of a cowed city
whose river has no bend
to return to Cap-Haitian—
saluting the honeyed fantasies of home
spawned by the simple need
of a man who can't build on the cunning of tomorrow

I whisper in his ear still open to thought
I hold his hand, scaled and aloof,
still greedy for the soles of other's fingertips
I say forget the cannons
and the piece of earth that exhales with no attention
my hants are vain
they dress in slips of purple and blue

today, we will sip evergreen plants
in the park where the Japanese teahouse sings
and we will berate any presumption
yours were days unspent.

-the end-

Mbali on Mama

Tony Medina

She looked like
a tree without
its leaves

a flower
without sun or water
unable to grow

I wanted
to put my arms
around her

and keep her
close to
me

but she wouldn't
let me get
too close

scared
that I would
be like her

a tree
without its
leaves

a day
without its
sun

and instead
whispered
sweet things

and kissed me
from across
the room

Viruses

Lamont B. Steptoe

invisible things
are killing us
viruses
are armies and bombs
we are murdered
genocided by a hidden hand
slowly we discover destruction
our tears and screams
beseeching heaven
for mercy

Winter

Carlos T. Mock

Everything is leveled to the same height by the snow.
White everywhere—the gentle blanket of death.
Lifeless trees trying to carry the burden,
As if sleeping to escape the death that surrounds them.

Peace—the peace created by the absence of noise.
Melting drops of snow feeding into the gentle streams.
Reflections of sunlight amplified by the white.
As if to make up for the lack of heat,
As if to bring us back another rainbow.

Just like there was an end to the great flood,
The rainbow reminds us of the coming spring.
Nature will be coming back to life—renewal
The start of another cycle and another chance.

Thousands of Angels

Anna Forbes

I said to my father once, "I'll try."
And he said, "That's all the angels can do."
Thinking of him, I sat down in the street
In front of the White House, in front of my world.

Facing the cameras, we started to name them
The lovers and friends who were torn from our lives
As the names of the dead rang out and embraced us
All my cold nervousness started to fade

I'm here for you, Bill. I'm bringing your anger
I'm here, Baby Luz, small and clear in my mind
Tell Mama Consuela I'm here with the fury
I felt on the day that I heard you'd both died

And, Robby, I smile as I wait for the handcuffs
I'm hearing your cracks about great-looking cops
Your fabulous wit is still here to delight me
I borrow the courage to live with your style

Thousands of angels surrounding the White House
The millions of us who have already died
Call out in our voices for housing, protection,
Medicine, food and no more genocide

Jamaal, keep me safe as my body's dragged from here
Brenda, stay with me and help me to shine
Keesha, come chant with us as, for the living,
We press the demands that will keep us alive.

Let's Confront AIDS

Dennis Brutus

Let's talk openly about AIDS,
about the pain and grief
about the anger and fear
about the deep sense of loss

Let's confront this dread scourge:
sing songs about the pain it brought
write poems of how it made life more dear
how it exposed the ugliness of hate

Let's have festivals to challenge AIDS
write books that record our response
have parades that defy the bigots
Come, let's talk openly about AIDS.

December 16, 1993
Boulder, CO

Contributors

Ifeanyi Ajaegbo is a conflict management and development expert working in the Niger Delta region of Nigeria. He won the 2005 Africa Regional Prize for the Commonwealth Short Story Competition. He was also in the British Council Crossing Borders writing program.

Joop Bersee was born in the Netherlands. His first English poems were published in 1993 in South Africa, and later in various magazines, anthologies, and e-zines in the UK, US, Canada, and India (in English and Malayalam translation). He has self-published a number of publications and is Editor of *Southern Rain Poetry:* (www.southernrainpoetry.com).

Reginald Dwayne Betts is a poet and student at Prince George's Community College. A Cave Canem fellow, his poetry has appeared in several journals, including *Poet Lore*. He also co-founded and runs YoungMenRead, Inc., a book club for teenage boys.

Tara Betts is a Cave Canem alum and an MFA candidate at New England College. Her writing has appeared in *ROLE CALL*, *Gathering Ground, Black Writing from Chicago: In the World, Not of It?, Bum Rush the Page*, and other publications. She also appeared on

HBO's "Def Poetry Jam." To learn more about her work, visit www.tarabetts.net.

Dennis Brutus has been called "the singing voice of South African Poetry." Shot by South African police during the Apartheid era, he was sentenced to forced labor on the infamous Robben Island, where he broke stones with Nelson Mandela for his efforts in banning South Africa from the Olympics because of its racial policies. Brutus is known as a premier global activist battling policies of the World Trade Organization, International Monetary Fund, and World Bank. He has authored fifteen books. The most recent are *leafdrift* (Whirlwind Press), a poetry collection spanning nearly twenty years of writing, and *The Dennis Brutus Reader* (Haymarket Publishers), a collection of poetry, prose, and speeches.

James E. Cherry is the author of *Shadow of Light*, a forthcoming novel (London: Serpents Tail, 2007). His fiction has appeared courtesy of *Shooting Star Review*, the *Exchange*, *Xavier Review*, *Nommo*, *360 Degrees*, and others.

Kimberly A. Collins is a doctoral student in English at Howard University. Ms. Collins is also the author of a collection of poetry, *Slightly Off Center*, and her writings appear in *Black Poets of the Deep South*, *In The Tradition*, *The Nubian Gallery*, *NOBO Journal of African American Dialogue*, *Theorizing Black Feminism*, *Catalyst*, and *Essence*.

Curtis L. Crisler is a Limited-Term Lecturer at Indiana Purdue Fort Wayne (IPFW). He has a forthcoming book from Front Street Press, *Tough Boy Sonatas*. He has recently published in *Elixir*, *Re)verb*, *The Ringing Ear: Anthology* (forthcoming), *L'Intrigue: Nature Anthology*, *Attic* (all forthcoming), *The Fourth River*, and *Only the Sea Keeps: Poetry of the Tsunami*.

Terry M. Dugan worked as a clinical trials coordinator and behavioral researcher in AIDS and oncology for 18 years. Most recently, she was a research scientist at Columbia University School of Physicians and Surgeons' HIV Center for Clinical and Behavioral Research (NY). She is also working on a chapbook, *The Saint Factory*.

Patricia Eldridge is 34 years old. She has a 10-year-old son. Patricia is a member of Trinity United Church of Christ in Chicago, IL, where she works in the HIV/AIDS Support Ministry. She has spoken at many different churches, organizations, as well as universities and seminaries. Patricia is currently working on her first book, entitled "Not My Will."

Anna Forbes writings have appeared in the *AIDS and Public Policy Journal, AIDS Policy and Law,* POZ, *Harvard Health Policy Review, The New York Times, Newsweek,* and other journals and periodicals. She has also contributed to anthologies, including the last two editions of *Our Bodies Ourselves,* and is the author of eight children's books on HIV/AIDS.

Ebony Golden currently resides in Durham, NC. She earned an MFA in Poetry from American University. Her poems appear in *WarpLand, Black Arts Quarterly,* and *The Ringing Ear: Black Poets Lean South* (forthcoming). Her poetry chapbook, *the sweet smell of juju funk,* was published by betty's daughter. To book a performance or workshop, please visit www.myspace.com/mamashieroglyphics.

Myronn Hardy is the author of the book of poems, *Approaching the Center.* His poems have appeared in *Ploughshares, Tampa Review,*

Callaloo, Many Mountains Moving, and *Third Coast.* He lives in New York City.

Diane Harriford is a free Black woman living in New York City and Poughkeepsie, New York. She teaches sociology at an upstate New York college.

Chanell Harris is a graduate of the MFA in Creative Writing program at Chicago State University. She served as Poetry Editor of the 2005 issue of *WarpLand.* Her poems will appear in the *Louisiana English Journal,* focusing on Hurricane Katrina. She assisted with the poetry anthology, *Dream of a Word* (Tia Chucha Press, 2006).

Duriel E. Harris is a co-founder of the Black Took Collective and a Poetry Editor for *Obsidian III.* Extending the multi-vocal experimentation of *Drag* (Elixir Press, 2003), her first book, Harris is currently at work on AMNESIAC, a media arts project. A Cave Canem fellow and recent MacDowell Colony resident, Harris teaches poetry at St. Lawrence University in upstate New York.

Melanie Henderson, 5th-generation native of Washington, DC, earned a B.A. in English & Spanish from Howard University and is a MBA candidate at Trinity University. Her poetry appears in *Drumvoices Revue, WarpLand, X Magazine* (London, UK), *Beltway Poetry Quarterly,* and *The Washington Informer.* Her visual art is available at www.cafepress.com/jalemdesigns.

Nancy Jackson is an MA candidate in Education at National Louis University. In her professional life, she is an educator, community organizer, and community-based educational activist. She has been published on numerous occasions by the Chicago Literary Exchange, Strong Coffee, the Chicago Community Trust-Children, and Youth and Families Initiative.

Roy Jacobstein's latest book of poetry, *A Form of Optimism* (University Press of New England, 2006), won the Samuel French Morse Prize, selected by Lucia Perillo. His previous book, *Ripe*, won the Felix Pollak Prize. His poetry appears in many literary publications as well as *Literature: Reading Fiction, Poetry & Drama* (McGraw-Hill, 2006).

Fred Joiner is a poet living in Washington, DC's historic Anacostia neighborhood. He works as a Systems Administrator for a small progressive consulting company. His still-untitled chapbook will be self-published this year.

Alan King has been published in *WarpLand*, *Inkstains Literary Magazine*, whimperbang.com, and *When Words Become Flesh: An Anthology of New Generation Poetry*. His self-published book, *Transfer*, is available at www.myspace.com/bustransfer.

Fredrick Douglas Knowles (Yesod) is a Poet-Educator-Activist. His publications include *Martin Luther King Jr. Anthology* (Yale UP 2003), and *Folio*, a Southern Connecticut State University literary magazine (2005). He has performed at the East Haddam Stage Company of Connecticut (2004) and the 13th Annual Acacia Group Conference at California State University.

Octavia McBride-Ahebee gives, for the most part, voice to women who historically have not been heard: African women, women in refugee camps, women who are victims of civil war, women who are new immigrants and isolated, rural women who battle such health challenges as breast cancer and obstetric fistula.

Stephen Mead is a published artist/writer living in northeastern New York. A resume and samples of his artwork can be seen in the portfolio section of www.absolutearts.com. Mr. Mead has several e-books and videos online, many of which are related to HIV concerns. Other merchandise by the artist can be found at www.lulu.com/stephenmead.

Tony Medina is the author of twelve books, the most recent of which are *Committed to Breathing* (Third World Press, 2003) and *Follow-up Letters to Santa from Kids Who Never Got a Response* (Just Us Books, 2003). Assistant Professor of Creative Writing at Howard University, Medina's work is featured in over thirty anthologies and two CD compilations. He divides his time between New York City and Washington, DC.

Dante Micheaux is an emerging poet who resides in New York City.

Carlos T. Mock, MD, is the author of *Borrowing Time: A Latino Sexual Odyssey* (Floricanto Press, 2003). The American Library Association Round Table nominated him for a Stonewall Award, and he is the upcoming author of *The Mosaic Virus*. For more info: www.carlostmock.com, www.pinkagenda.com.

Ruth O'Callaghan has been widely published and is one of five poets featured in *Take Five '06* (Shoestring Press). She has been an invited guest reader at various venues in the UK and abroad. Also a playwright, her work has been presented at the Finborough, Oval House, Soho, and Old Red Lion Theatres, and she amongst the final playwrights selected by *The Plays The Thing*.

Dike Okoro, a poet and essayist, is finishing a PhD at the University of Wisconsin at Milwaukee. His collection of poetry, *Dance of the Heart*, is forthcoming in 2006 (Malthouse Press, London & Lagos).

Ayo Oyeku is an up-and-coming African writer who has published two short stories with a Nigerian publisher. Some of his poems have appeared in foreign anthologies. He is from the Osun state in Nigeria and is an undergraduate student. Presently, he is working on his first novel.

Deborah Poe's writing has recently appeared, or is forthcoming, in *Drunken Boat* (as a finalist for the Panliterary Awards), *Triplopia*, *Snow Monkey*, and *Anemone Sidecar*. Her chapbook „clitoris„ „vulva„ „penis„ and *(W(e)a(St) Solo* were published in April and October 2004 (furniture press). One of her poems was recently nominated for a Pushcart Prize.

Gerald Ribeiros (1951-2002) was born and raised in New Bedford, MA. He emerged from poverty, discrimination and drug addiction to become a highly respected advocate for drug treatment, an AIDS activist, and a community leader for social change.

Melanie Rivera is a teacher of language arts at Winston Middle School in Baltimore. A graduate of American University and a graduate student at Johns Hopkins, Melanie plans to pursue an MFA in Creative Writing and continue her work with poetry and social justice.

L. E. Scott is a poet/writer and frequent traveler to Africa. He is also the Australasian editor for *Kalimat*, an Arabic/English literary magazine based in Sydney, Australia. His latest collection of poems, *Bones*, was published in 2004 (Five Islands Press, Melbourne University, Australia). Scott was born in Georgia and currently resides in Wellington, New Zealand.

Evie Shockley is the author of *The Gorgon Goddess* (2001) and *a half-red sea* (2006), both with Carolina Wren Press. Her work also appears in numerous journals and anthologies. Shockley is a Cave Canem fellow and has received a variety of residencies and scholarships in support of her poetry. She teaches at Rutgers University.

Beth Snyder was born in Philadelphia, PA, and received her BA from Sarah Lawrence College. In 2001, she earned an MFA in Writing from the School of the Art Institute of Chicago. She works at Northwestern University as a senior writer in development and is enrolled as a Visiting Scholar in the Creative Writing MA program.

Lamont B. Steptoe was born and raised in Pittsburgh, PA. Steptoe is a Vietnam veteran, photographer, publisher and author of eleven collections of poetry. His book, A *Long Movie of Shadows* won the 2005 American Book award, and he is the 2006 recipient of the Pew Fellowship for the Arts in Poetry, a $50,000 award. His latest book is *Crowns and Halos* (Whirlwind Press).

Truth Thomas is an emerging musician and poet from Washington, DC. His poetry has appeared or is forthcoming in *African Voices, Art Times, Lorraine & James, Main Channel Voices, Poet Lore, Poetalk, The New Verse News, The Henniker Review, The Ringing Ear* (a Cave Canem anthology), *WarpLand, X-Magazine,* and other journals.

Randi Triant received her MFA in writing and literature from Bennington College. Her nonfiction and fiction have appeared most recently in *The Writer's Chronicle, Post Road,* and *Art & Understanding,* and her story "Starfish" won the Salt Flats Emerging Fiction Writer's competition.

Frank X. Walker is the author of *Affrilachia, Buffalo Dance: The Journey of York,* and *Black Box.* A founding member of the Affrilachian Poets and a Cave Canem Fellow, he received the 2005 Lannan Literary Fellowship for Poetry. In 2004, he won the Lillian Smith Book Award for *Buffalo Dance.*

Arisa White holds an MFA from the University of Massachusetts, Amherst. She is a recipient of the Archie D. and Bertha H. Walker Scholarship from the Fine Arts Work Center in Provincetown and was recently awarded a writing residency at the Atlantic Center for the Arts. She is a Cave Canem fellow. Her most recent work appears in *Gathering Ground: Cave Canem 10th Anniversary Reader*.

avery r. young, writer/educator/performance artist, has been a staple in the spoken word community since 1996. He has worked with the Imani Nina Theatre team, whose work centered on HIV/AIDS prevention. Mr. young edited *Abstractvision* and is a columnist for *Say What* magazine. He is the author of *lookin fo/words that rhyme: the un-spoken word of avery r. young* (FayeRic).

Permissions

Dennis Brutus, "Let's Confront Aids" and "HIV/AIDS," originally published in *leafdrift* (Whirlwind Press, 2005). Reprinted by permission of Dennis Brutus.

Ruth O'Callaghan, "Guatemalan Postcript," originally appears in *Sean Poetry Magazine* (Issue 22, January 2005). Reprinted by permission of Ruth O'Callaghan.

Duriel Harris, "Gravity" and "Brown Sugar," originally appear in *Drag* (Elixir Press, 2003). Reprinted by permission of Duriel Harris.

Roy Jacobstein, "HIV Needs Assessment," originally published in *Prairie Schooner*. Reprinted by permission of Roy Jacobstein.

Octavia McBride, "The Japanese Teahouse," originally published in *Assuming Voices* (Lit Pot Press, 2003). Reprinted by permission of Octavia McBride.

Carlos Mock, "Winter," originally appears in the novel, *Borrowing Time: A Latino Sexual Odyssey* (Floricanto Press, 2003). Reprinted by permission of Carlos Mock.

Frank X. Walker, "We Real Crunk," originally appears in *black box poems* (Old Cove Press, 2006). Reprinted by permission of Frank X. Walker.

Acknowledgements

We are grateful to all the authors in this collection and to all the individuals who submitted pieces. We want to especially thank Haki Madhubuti, Quraysh Ali Lansana, and Gwendolyn Mitchell for guidance and support to see this collection come to fruition, and Kim Foote for editorial input.

This collection was driven by the support of participants from the Gwendolyn Brooks Conference for Black Literature and Creative Writing at Chicago State University over the last three years. The enthusiasm witnessed at these conferences has highlighted the necessity of this work. The partnership with the Chicago Department of Public Health has been a tremendous value in the development and accuracy of this collection.

For all those individuals living with HIV or AIDS, we are in the battle with you and want you to know this collection was put together not from sympathy but from a deep desire to stand tall, for and with our brothers and sisters.

Hunter's Thank You's

Peace and blessings. My appreciation runs deep from all the individuals who have supported me throughout my life. I thank my blood and God-given family. My parents, John and Mary Deloney, have always given me an anchor in this world. Rodney E. Pryor, my partner, has encouraged me to live my full life.

Randall's Thank You's

Hunter and Becky, this was a blessing I needed. Thanks also to the inmates of Roxbury Correctional Facility in Hagerstown, MD. If I made it out, so can you.

Becky's Thank You's

Randall, many props. Thanks also to Susan Kosoff, Diane Harriford, Ethelbert Miller, Cornell Coley, Regie Gibson, Macdara Woods, Vijay Seshadri, and Sonia Sanchez.

Editors' Bios

Randall Horton, poet, is originally from Birmingham, AL. His first poetry collection, *The Definition of Place* (Main Street Rag, 2006), was a finalist in Main Street Rag's Poetry Book Award. His poetry has appeared in *Dance the Guns to Silence: 100 Poems Inspired by Ken Saro-Wiwa* and in *Tigertail, Versal,* and several other literary magazines. He was Assistant Editor of *Dream of a Word* (Tia Chucha Press, 2006) and is a former editor of *WarpLand* (Fall 2005). Randall was educated at both Howard University and the University of the District of Columbia, and received an MFA in Creative Writing, emphasis in poetry, from Chicago State University. He was awarded a 2005 Archie D. and Bertha H. Walker Foundation Summer Scholarship to attend the Fine Arts Work Center at Provincetown. He is also a Cave Canem fellow. Currently, he resides in Albany, New York, where he is a doctoral student at SUNY Albany.

M. L. Hunter was born in Lexington, MS, in 1967 and grew up in Indianapolis, IN. He has worked in the HIV/AIDS field since 1994. He currently lives in Chicago and is the Communication and Policy Administrator for the Chicago Department of Public Health's STD/HIV/AIDS Policy and Program. He is also currently completing an MFA in Creative Writing at Chicago State University, emphasis in poetry. A natural educator, Hunter motivates individuals to step into their own power. He has written articles for newspapers and magazines in the Indianapolis and Chicago areas. Hunter is working on his first collection of poetry, tentatively entitled "When I Was Mine," which examines black, gay, HIV life.

Becky Thompson, PhD, is the author of *A Promise and A Way of Life*, *Mothering without a Compass*, *A Hunger So Wide and So Deep*, and *When the Center is on Fire: Passionate Social Theory for Troubled Times* (forthcoming, with Diane Harriford.) She has been awarded fellowships from the Rockefeller Foundation, the American Association for University Women, the NEH, the Ford Foundation, Political Research Associates, and the Gustavus Myers Award for Outstanding Books on Human Rights in North America. Her poems have recently appeared in *WarpLand*, *Amandla*, *Illuminations*, *The Teacher's Voice*, and *In Women's Hands*. Becky speaks nationally and internationally on multiracial feminism, trauma and embodiment, and human rights. She has taught at Duke University, Wesleyan University, and the University of Massachusetts, and currently teaches African American Studies and Sociology at Simmons College in Boston.